Postcard view of Kaiserstrasse c. 1905. Public domain.

Jews of Kaiserstrasse

MAINZ, GERMANY

By
Michael Stowell Phillips

Published by JewishGen, Inc.
An Affiliate of The Museum of Jewish Heritage—
A Living Memorial to the Holocaust
New York, NY

Jews of Kaiserstrasse
© 2020 by Michael Stowell Phillips
All rights reserved.
First Printing: November 2020, Cheshvan-Kislev 5780

Editor and Project Coordinator: Victoria Robson
Book and Cover Design: Nina Schwartz/ImpulseGraphics.com

Published by JewishGen, Inc.
An Affiliate of the Museum of Jewish Heritage
A Living Memorial to the Holocaust
36 Battery Place, New York, NY 10280

JewishGen, Inc. is not responsible for inaccuracies or omissions in this original work and makes no representations regarding its accuracy.

The mission of the JewishGen organization is to produce a translation of the original work, and we cannot verify the accuracy of statements or alter facts cited.

Printed in the United States of America by Lightning Source, Inc.

Library of Congress Control Number (LCCN): 2020948146
ISBN: 978-1-939561-47-3 (hard cover: 160 pages, alk. paper)

Cover Images:
Front cover, above: Kennkarte (identity card) of Carl Theodor Frank, issued 1939.
Source: Central Archive for the Study of the History of the Jews in Germany.
Below: Karl and Sonja Gutmann (née Herzfeld), mid-1930s, Michael Stowell Phillips Archive.
Background: Aerial view of Kaiserstrasse in 1892, public domain. Source: Wikipedia.org.
Back cover, above left: Rudolf and William Frank, c.1894. Courtesy of Lisa Wasserman Weissberg.
Right: The author's grandmother, Milly (Amalie) Gutmann, c.1912, Michael Stowell Phillips Archive.

Contents

Foreword I

In this remarkable study Michael S. Phillips presents a vignette of Jewish experience in one street in Mainz in the 1930s and 40s. His work opens the reader's eyes to the systematic stigmatisation, persecution, deportation to the camps and murder there of the Jewish population in Nazi Germany and the countries they occupied during those tragic years.

His starting place is the escape of his Jewish grandmother, Milly Schwarz, from Berlin in 1939. A widow in her forties, her flight from persecution was only made possible by the payment of huge sums of money to secure a passport and permission and sponsorship by close Jewish friends settled in England, the family of Alice Morreau. She had to leave much behind, including property and a profitable business that she had managed successfully for many years following the death of her husband. She could no longer visit her childhood home, a substantial house at 32 Kaiserstrasse in Mainz, where her mother Auguste and sister Anna were living until the three of them fled together for England.

Milly Schwarz settled first in Manchester and then in Guildford, Surrey where she worked as a school cook. She brought up her grandson, Michael, from the age of two almost entirely on her own after Michael's parents divorced. Sadly her daughter, Michael's mother Anneliese was to take her own life six years later. This book is to some measure a tribute to Milly, who often talked about the house on Kaiserstrasse, which she loved, the street and their friends and neighbours who lived nearby.

After her death, Michael decided to research the history of the wealthy Jewish families with prosperous businesses—similar to his own—that lived on the street shortly before and during World War

Two. He has visited Mainz several times and has been welcomed by local researchers, neighbours, a former teacher from the girls' high school on the corner that Milly attended, and others who supported the project. He found many properties, including his grandmother's house, had been flattened by Allied bombing during the war and replaced by modern office blocks. The original buildings that remain are now protected due to their historical architectural importance.

While the Jewish community that once lived on Kaiserstrasse has been destroyed along with many of their former homes, small brass bricks embedded in the pavement preserve the memory of individual residents murdered by the Nazi regime. Images of these 'Stumbling Stones' are included in the book, which also contains photographs and other illustrations that bring the information Michael discovered to life. The fates of the individuals featured in this book are indicative of what was happening to Jews everywhere in Nazi-controlled territory, which resulted in the near elimination of Jewish families and communities in Europe. This is a work of scrupulous scholarship and family devotion.

Rosalind Wilson (née Morreau)
Retired peace education facilitator and higher education lecturer, active member of Amnesty International, poet, and granddaughter of Alice Morreau.

Foreword II

On 9 May 2018, three 'stolpersteine' were laid in the pavement outside 32 Kaiserstrasse in Mainz. The small brass plaques serve as individual memorials to the lives of Auguste Gutmann and her adult children Anna and Karl Gutmann, former residents of the house who were murdered by the Nazi regime because they were Jewish.

Auguste's oldest daughter Milly Schwarz survived the Nazi atrocities committed during the Second World War. She fled to England in 1939, where she lived out the rest of her days. She died in 1977 aged 82. Her grandson Michael S. Phillips attended the stolpersteine ceremony, as did I. I could see that it was a deeply emotional event for him.

Only after Milly's death, Michael felt he could investigate his family Jewish roots. He began visiting Mainz and the city archives to conduct research. With the help of local historians with whom he soon became good friends, he was able to reconstruct the fate of Auguste, Anna and Karl. He also discovered more stolpersteine in Kaiserstrasse. The street where his grandmother grew up is a large boulevard lined with big four-storey houses built between 1880 and 1914 in the typical Wilhelminian style. There's a pretty green park running down the centre. Before they were forced to leave due to Nazi persecution, many Jewish families had resided in these grand residential buildings, which also housed business premises, offices and medical practices.

As Michael discovered, several of his family's neighbours were deported by the Gestapo to concentration camps and murdered, while others managed to emigrate to overseas. This book is a compilation of an amazing amount of information, photographic evidence and documents he has found that describe the fate of hundreds of individuals. However, it tells more than just the story of Jews that lived on this particular street. Kaiserstrasse serves as a microcosm for the fate of the 2,600-strong Jewish community that was living in Mainz in 1933, when Nazi harassment began in earnest.

The destruction of the Jewish community in this neighbourhood and in the wider city was a human tragedy and has resulted in an irreversible economic, social and cultural loss to the city. Michael's book is an impressive memorial to the Jews of Kaiserstrasse and, furthermore, to all the Jews of Mainz and beyond.

Dr. Hedwig Brüchert
Historian, researcher at the Institute for Regional Historical Studies at Mainz University, and author of several books on the Jewish history of Mainz.

Chapter 1. Escape

On 8 March 1939, my grandmother, Milly Schwarz, was finally granted permission to travel. Her German passport and exit visa were stamped with a red capital 'J' indicating she was Jewish. She had paid almost 1 million Reichsmarks, the equivalent then to $400,000 or £87,000[1]—an extraordinary sum—as a capital tax applied to all Jews that wanted to leave Germany. A businesswoman living in Berlin, she had been trying to escape Nazi Germany for years. All her previous attempts, including to move her textile company to England, had been denied.

Her documents arrived just in time. A week later, the Nazi regime occupied the rest of Czechoslovakia it had yet to annex. Nazi Party leader and Führer, Adolf Hitler had already instigated the takeover of Austria a year earlier, and was poised to invade Poland at the beginning of September, an act that would trigger Britain's declaration of war with Germany and the start of the Second World War.

That April, aged 45 and having lived her entire life in Germany, Milly fled. The owner, president and chief executive of Schwarz & Son, a large business with textile factories in Greiz in eastern Germany and Riga, Latvia, she was a wealthy and accomplished woman. She was prohibited from taking any of her money with her and was forced to abandon most of her possessions, as well as a substantial house, and her profitable business. She had run the company since 1925, when she inherited a majority stake from her husband Walter Schwarz. He was killed when their chauffeur-driven car crashed. They had only been married five years.

My grandmother seldom spoke about the years before World War II. As a child I didn't think to ask her, and as an adult I did not wish to upset her by asking painful questions about such a sad time in her life. But I assume her mother Auguste Gutmann and her sister Anna Gutmann travelled the 600 or so kilometres east from their home town Mainz, which sits on the Rhine in the heart of German wine growing country, to join her in Berlin. Possibly they left without reporting their movements or obtaining permission. I suspect the three of them then set off by train for the Netherlands and travelled by boat to England from the Hook of Holland. There is no record of their route or their reliance on support from any Jewish charity. Milly would have had sufficient funds to pay their way.

Milly's younger brother Karl, who, excluded from job opportunities in Mainz because he was Jewish, had already left Germany in the mid-1930s for Riga, where he assisted the Schwarz textile operations. There he was protected—for a short while—from the escalating social, political and economic persecution of Jewish people in Nazi Germany epitomised by anti-Jewish riots in November 1938. During Kristallnacht, mobs attacked Jewish businesses, property and synagogues abetted by the police and ratcheting up unchecked anti-Jewish violence in a horrible foreshadowing of what was to come.

Milly, Auguste and Anna arrived in Manchester where they were taken in by the family of Alice Morreau, the sister of Milly's best and lifelong friend Berthe Goetz. Marcus, Alice's late husband, had been a successful businessman involved in the textile and, to a lesser extent, wine trades. Milly was reunited with her 18-year-old daughter Anneliese (my mother) and her son Max Walter (known as Walter), who was a year younger. Milly had sought to shield them from the increasingly savage anti-Semitism in Germany by sending them abroad for their education.

Sponsored by the Morreau family, Walter attended boarding school at Dartington Hall from May 1933. In 1939, the Morreau's generosity extended to sponsoring my grandmother, Walter and

Anneliese, who made her way from Switzerland where she had been attending the International School in Geneva, having already spent time at Dartington in 1935, as well as at a private German school in Ascona, where Milly kept a sizeable villa (either owned or rented). Auguste and Anna, who were without British sponsors, could not stay. They travelled on to Riga to join Karl. The Schwarz factories there were still generating income and they believed they would be safe among a growing community of German exiles. That was not to be the case.

My grandmother was a tough woman. She was very modern for her time and not shy. One striking example of her unwillingness to give in is the courtcase she launched in the 1930s against Dr Otto Olwein, her mandatory Nazi party business partner, and her non-Jewish brother-in-law, a Nazi-sympathiser, when they sought to exploit Aryanisation laws to take control of her company. Remarkably, she won. Using his Nazi Party connections, it was Olwein who helped facilitate Milly's escape. It was not altruistic. In return, he finally succeeded in stealing her business.

Although safe, the transition to life in England could not have been easy. She settled in a house in Guildford (Surrey), an environment in stark contrast to material comfort that she left behind. She had also left many of her friends, extended family members and the places that were significant to her, importantly 32 Kaiserstrasse, her mother's house and the place where Milly said she had enjoyed a very happy and loving childhood. Middle-aged and widowed, now living in a foreign country with two teenage children, she had to begin again.

Childhood

Amalie (Milly) Gutmann was named after her paternal grandmother (Amalie Gutmann née Adler), who died a year before Milly was born on 21 September 1894. She was the oldest child of Ferdinand Gutmann, a wine merchant, and Auguste (née Mayer) from Alzey. Milly attended the Höhere Mädchenschule, a Mainz state high school, along with her sister, Anna, who was six years younger, and members of her extended family, as well as the daughters of many Jewish families who lived on Kaiserstrasse.

Around 1908 the family moved from 1 Kirchplatz (later renamed Bonifaziusplatz) in Mainz, where my grandmother was born, to 32 Kaiserstrasse, a grand building on a magnificent street big enough to function as a family home and business premises. Indeed the adjacent three properties (26, 28 and 30) housed the H. Sichel Söhne wine operation run by the founder's three sons. Most of that family left before the war for France, England and the USA. One of the sons, Peter Max Ferdinand Sichel (b. 1922), returned in 1945 as a captain in the US Army to participate in the liberation of Mainz. He found the buildings burned to the ground but the cellars untouched, as recounted in his book *The Secrets of My Life: Vintner, Prisoner, Soldier, Spy.*[2] They were apparently large enough to hold one million litres of wine, which was returned to the family, sufficient to revive their business. Post-war, it began to produce the popular brand Blue Nun.

Like many Jewish families, the Gutmanns had lived in the area for generations. I have traced my ancestors as far back as their move from Fürth in Bavaria (next door to Nuremberg / Nürnberg) to Gross-Rohrheim in the 18th century, about 40 kilometres south of Mainz and the town where Milly's father Ferdinand was born in 1858.

Ferdinand's father Samuel was active in the wine trade, but it was Ferdinand's cousin Max Gutmann, who was instrumental in establishing the Gutmann wine business in Mainz.[3] Born in Hahn on 26 May 1824, he probably grew up in Gross-Rohrheim and was possibly already producing wine in Mainz before he married Rosalie Mayer in 1852.[4] She was born in the city on 6 April 1834. In the same year Max married he became a citizen of Mainz. Between 1854 and 1867, Max and Rosalie had 10 children. During this time he entered into partnership with Eduard Saarbach as a wine wholesaler based at 41 Grosse Bleiche, another grand street where Max's family also lived.[5]

Sometime before 1870, the business partners separated and the company split into two, but the connection between the families did not end. Eduard's son August (1854-1912) married Max's daughter Johanna (1863-1940), known as Jenny.

Around the same time Max formed his new business, Rosalie was listed in the commercial register as her husband's managing clerk. The company was based at 12 1/10 Petersstrasse. It is fair to assume the company was doing very well. The labels on its bottles carried the endorsement "Grand Ducal Court Supplier" and "Court Supplier to the Czar".

By 1883, the business was based at 32 Boulevard, soon to be renamed Kaiserstrasse. Upon Max's death on 15 December 1896, ownership passed to his eldest son Siegfried (b. 11 March 1854) and his cousin Ferdinand, Milly's father, who became company secretary. Ferdinand was already a 'confidential clerk' and had the authority to sign cheques. Rosalie, Max's widow, assumed the role of general manager. Just before Max passed away, the business had expanded to trade in not just wine but also spirits. Max left a fortune to his widow and children, as suggested by this clipping I found in the Australian press, detailing his son Joseph Gutmann's inheritance. Like many of Max's children, Joseph, who was born in 1860, had emigrated.

The Heir to a Fortune

Sassafras Gully, Saturday.
A settler named Gutmann, who resides near the Olinda township, has come into a fortune of about £13,000 [More than $1 million in today's money] from his father, who has lately died in Germany.
Source: The Melbourne Argus, Monday 22 March 1890

When Max died, Ferdinand had been married to Auguste for three years and they had one daughter, Milly, who was toddler. In 1897, Ferdinand became a citizen of Mainz and his son Karl was born. A second daughter, Anna, was born in 1900. Shortly after, in 1901, Rosalie died, followed in 1904 by her son Siegfried, who was unmarried and had no heirs. It seems that Ferdinand was left in sole charge of the business and around 1908, he started to use 32 Kaiserstrasse as a family home. While Max's children never lived there, many of them resided in the same neighbourhood.

Kaiserstrasse was not Ferdinand's home for long. In 1910, he died of cancer and is buried in the New Jewish Cemetery in Mainz, as are Max and Rosalie. Auguste took charge of the wine wholesale business, while also raising her three children. A woman playing an instrumental role in business is a theme of the Gutmann family. Some people may attribute it to strength of character, but I think they simply had no choice.

At the beginning of the First World War, Auguste was listed as the owner of the Max Gutmann Company, along with Chary (Zacharias) Gochsheimer and her only brother Paul Mayer, a banker who lived on a street close to Kaiserstrasse.

At the end of that war and the defeat of Germany and the oc-cupation of the area by French forces, like many Mainz residents, Auguste let rooms in her house to French army officers. Again she probably had no choice, but it did allow her to generate addition-al income. The cost of maintaining the building alone would have been a burden. Her daughter Milly and her future husband Walter Schwarz were already courting. He sent her love notes written in formal old German. Milly resided at 32 Kaiserstrasse until they mar-ried on 11 May 1920 in a ceremony probably held at the house.

Walter came from a prominent and wealthy Jewish family in Greiz—his grandfather Samuel sat on the town council—a small town about 400 kilometres from Mainz, not far from Germany's border with the Czech Republic. Married and living in Greiz, Milly's circumstances changed dramatically. Walter's textile business occu-pied several large premises, which employed several hundred staff and supported the family's luxurious lifestyle. She gave birth to my mother on 6 April 1921, and my uncle on 15 December 1922. She had access to funds with which she could support her mother, brother and sister. While Schwarz & Son continued to thrive, in the face of rising anti-Semitism, Auguste struggled throughout the 1920s to keep her wine business afloat. It ceased to operate from about 1933 onwards, crippled by punitive anti-Jewish legislation and attitudes,[6] which are likely to have prevented Auguste and Karl, who was by then a co-owner, from procuring wine to sell. In contrast, the suc-cess of the textile factories under my grandmother's management provided her with the huge amount of funds she needed to pay the Nazi regime in order to leave Germany.

Friends

Alice Morreau (b.1880 in Calais; d.1971 Guildford) and Berthe Goetz (b. 1886 in Calais; d. 1971 in London), born Weinmann, were very important figures in my grandmother's life, and, her survival. They were both strong-willed and independently minded women. Alice and Berthe spoke French to each other—when they left Germany as young women, the Weinmanns lived in Calais in France before arriving in England—and German with my grandmother and English to me. Like my grandmother, Alice and Berthe were Jewish and brought up in a tight-knit community, but they were not religious. I remember many Christmases spent at Alice's house.

I have often asked myself why Alice, who sponsored my grandmother to come to England, and her son Rene, who sponsored my uncle, and her daughter Madeleine who took responsibility for my mother, were so extremely generous to my grandmother. I believe the answer is that the Morreaus were distant relations of Milly's mother's family who also came from the Alzey area. They were also bound by friendship. My grandmother and Berthe, who was a decade or so older were best friends from the time when Milly was a teenager until Berthe died. It is almost certain that Berthe introduced Milly to her future husband Walter. Berthe's mother-in-law and Walter's mother were sisters. After Walter died in 1925, Milly, the mother of two children under five years old, suffered a severe breakdown. She left Greiz and took my mother and uncle to live in Berlin, close to Berthe and her husband Alfred—the same house she'd be forced to abandon 14 years later.

When Milly and her children arrived in England, not only did Alice open her home to the three of them before they moved south to Guildford, living initially with Alice's daughter-in-law, but she also supported Milly financially. Until a year after Alice died in 1973, she provided Milly with £500 a year—a lot of money still even in the 1970s and significantly more in the forties.

During the war, Milly cooked at a small local school, acted as a local warden and I know she had some interaction with German prisoners of war detained at Merrow Downs less than a mile from her home.

In December 1940, Milly received the last communication from her sister Anna in Riga, where she was probably sharing a house with their mother Auguste, brother Karl and his wife Sonia and their little boy, Joe, born in 1937.

The Cable and Wireless telegram was typed in rather garbled English, but I understand the gist of it to be:

Best wishes to [Max] Walter, Karl is working hard to learn
weaving, Sonja is juggling being a mother and housekeeper,
Anny is hoping to find work.
Kisses.
Anny Gutmann

Nazi forces invaded Latvia in July 1941 and immediately began murdering the Jewish and Roma populations.[7] Those Jews not killed in mass executions that autumn were forcibly moved into ghettos established in the Maskavas Forstate neighbourhood of Riga. The ghetto existed for more than two years and housed Jews from Latvia, Germany, Austria and Czechoslovakia. Upon its liquidation in mid-1943, the remaining residents were sent to Kaiserwald concentration camp, built that year, to work as slave labour. The camp was evacuated in 1944 in the face of the Red Army advance. During this time, the Schwarz & Son factories in Greiz were appropriated to produce German military uniforms, including for SS paramilitaries.

As soon as the war ended, my grandmother tried to find out exactly what happened to her mother and siblings, and the textile operations. Alice's daughter Madeleine helped her in her quest, but it was difficult to make headway as Latvia then was part of the Soviet Union. My research indicates that by 1942, Auguste, Anna, Sonia and Joe, who would have been only five, were murdered in Riga. Karl was sent to the Russian front and died in a soviet labour camp in 1945/46.

My grandmother was successful in claiming modest compensation from the West German government for the loss of her property and company (a claim she was obliged to pursue with her once 'business partner' Otto Olwein). As a former business owner and chief executive of a German company, she also received a generous German pension. It was enough to pay my school fees and for her to send money to her son Max Walter, who had served in the British Army during the war and qualified as a doctor before he emigrated with his wife and first son to Canada. Once the Berlin Wall fell in 1989, I made my own successful claim for reparations. At the same time, Olwein made another claim on the company and failed.

Trauma

I believe trauma passes down the generations. My mother's life, which could have been very different, was unsettled from an early age, mired as it was by personal tragedy set against a backdrop of volatile political scene in Germany. Losses, such as the accidental death of her father when she was little, and then the orchestrated murders of her best friend Cornelius and close family members in the Nazi concentration camps, must have had a significant impact.

My mother was extremely bright. She met my father, Ronald Stowell Phillips, while studying economics (with a focus on sociology) at The London School of Economics (LSE) in the early 1940s. When the university was evacuated to Cambridge she continued her studies there and was an active committee member in the student union. My father, who was vocally supportive of the communist cause, was completing his PhD thesis at the LSE. He undoubtedly impressed Anneliese. Despite her mother's strong disapproval, they married in 1941. Upon graduation in 1943, with an upper-second degree, Anneliese began to work for the Workers' Educational Association in Nottingham. I was born a year later.

My grandmother looked after me frequently from around the time I was about six months old, and then permanently from when I was two. I was the first child she raised without the help of a nanny, cook or other household staff.

My parents' marriage was short-lived and they divorced on 1 September 1946.

I doubt my mother had the emotional or financial resources to care for a child. After the war, Anneliese lived in Oxford and earned a living by teaching. By 1951 she was living in rooms in Coventry. In the spring of that year, she travelled to Glasgow and killed herself by cutting her wrists. It was her second attempt.

It was only after my grandmother's death in 1977 at age 82 that I began my quest to learn about my ancestors. I have visited Mainz and Kaiserstrasse countless times as an adult, but only twice with my grandmother as a child. One memory sticks in my mind of a holiday we took when I was about eight shortly after my mother had died. I don't know why we went but I'm sure that was a factor. I stayed with my mother's former nanny, whose youngest son was my age, for a couple of weeks. She and my grandmother remained very close. My grandmother also remained friends with her former cook for the rest of her life.

Milly took me to Kaiserstrasse to show me where the house once stood. Bombed in 1942 by the British Royal Air Force (RAF), in its place stood a modernist block. However, the handsome facades of the few surviving properties on the street suggested its former glory. I cannot recall what my grandmother said about the street, beyond telling me that even the RAF had left their mark on the house, and I have no idea what she felt standing there once again. But I do know there was once a vibrant Jewish community of my grandmother's friends, family and neighbours living there, and now there is not.

It is important to me, but also a worthy task in itself to document how these families were forced to flee or were persecuted, imprisoned, hounded, attacked, robbed and transported from their homes and ultimately murdered. In the following pages I have attempted such a task.

Special Find

Researching the Gutmann family has been a long process. I've been helped in this task by Mainz-based historian Reinhard Frenzel, who has undertaken considerable research on what happened to the pupils of the Höhere Mädchenschule—by then the Frauenlob-Gymnasium—where he taught English.

I first met Reinhard 25 years ago, when he first showed me the school, the house where my grandmother was born at 1 Bonifazius-platz, and, Kaiserstrasse. At a much later date he asked me to help him find out more about the children of Max Gutmann's daughter Emma Neumann. Her daughter Louise Neumann lived in New York and survived the war, while her other daughter Margarete escaped to England. Reinhard believed Margarete's daughter Elsbeth Juda (née Goldstein) was living in London and asked me to investigate.

I exhausted all avenues before I decided to simply look for Elsbeth in the telephone directory. I found one E Juda living in London and wrote to her. To my astonishment, she telephoned me. And then, aged 99, she sent me an email. I mentioned this discovery to a family member, who it turned out, had known Elsbeth for 40 years, totally unaware that we were all linked.

Elsbeth, who died in 2014, was a well-known fashion and portrait photographer.[8] One of her more famous projects was to document artist Graham Sutherland as he painted a portrait of Winston Churchill, commissioned to celebrate his 80th birthday. Apparently the former British prime minister hated the portrait and it was never displayed and later destroyed. However, images from the shoot survive. Elsbeth donated her archive of it to the National Portrait Gallery in London.[9]

GEGRÜNDET 1853.

WEINGROSSHANDLUNG

MAX GUTMANN

HOF-
LIEFERANT

TELEGRAMME: FERNSPRECHER
MAX GUTMANN   NR. 412

REICHSBANK GIRO-KONTO.
POSTSCHECK-KONTEN:
FRANKFURT A.M. NR. 5502.
KÖLN A.RH. NR. 47734.

Fig. 1.1 Max Gutmann Wine Company Letterhead. Source: Michael S. Phillips Archive.

Fig. 1.2 Max Gutmann Wine Company Wine Bottle.
The business was based at 32 Boulevard, renamed Kaiserstrasse.
Source: Michael S. Phillips Archive.

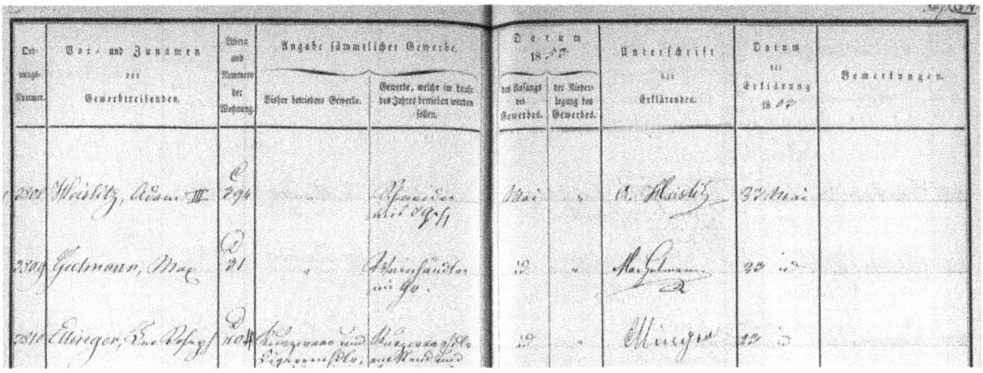

Fig. 1.3 Max Gutmann's signature, May 1853. Source: Mainz City Archives, Reference: 70/16327.

Fig. 1.4 Grave of Max and Rosalie Gutmann in the New Jewish Cemetery, Mainz. Source: Michael S. Phillips Archive.

Fig. 1.5 Johanna 'Jenny' Saarbach (née Gutmann). Jenny was Max Gutmann's eighth child. She married August Saarbach, the son of Max's business partner Eduard Saarbach. She died on 24 July 1940 at the Jewish Hospital aged 77. Source: Christine Meska Thorsrud, Jenny's granddaughter.

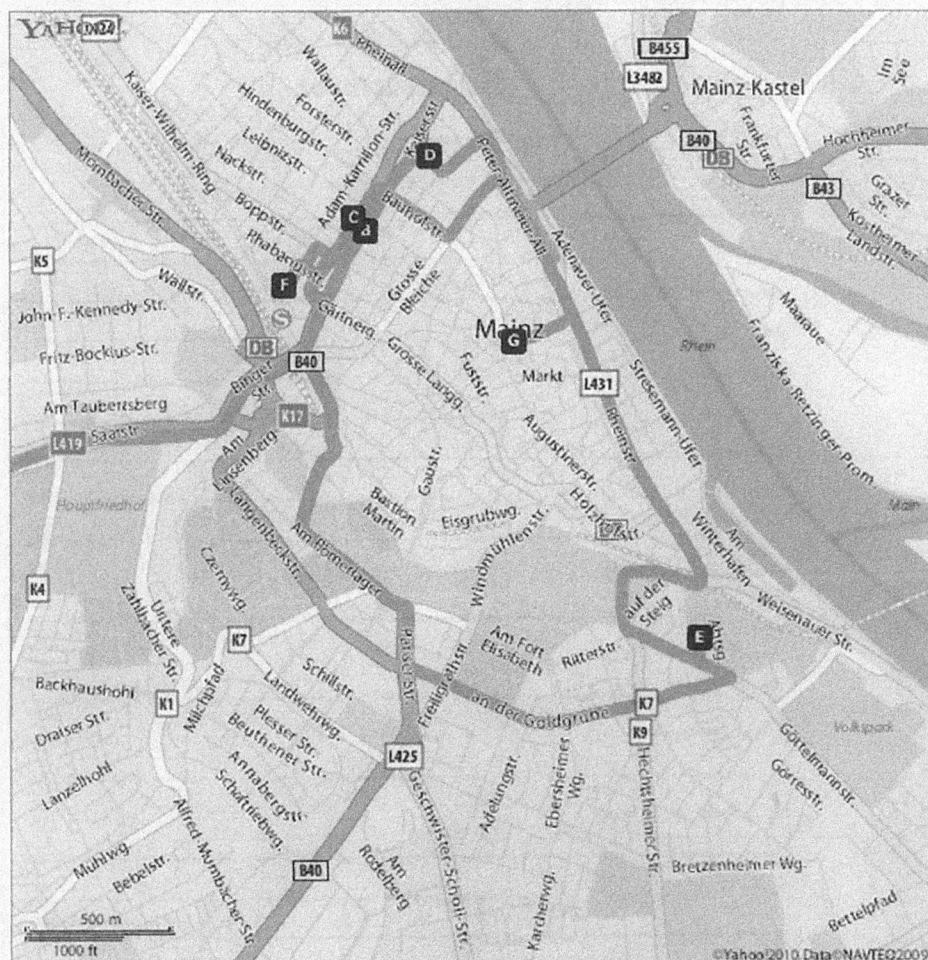

A	GONSENHEIMER STR.13, MAINZ	- Johanna Saarbach/GUTMANN lived here (off map down l419)
B	KAISER STR.27, MAINZ	- EMMA NEUMANN/GUTMANN lived here
C	KAISER STR.32, MAINZ	- MILLY & ALL MAX GUTMANN BROUGHT UP HERE/BORN HERE
D	ERNST-LUDWIG STR.10, MAINZ	- Dr.ELIZABETH MAYER/BING lived here
F	BONIFAZIUS STR.1, MAINZ	- MILLY GUTMANN BORN HERE

Fig. 1.6 Gutmann homes. Using Google Maps, I have created a map of locations in and around Kaiserstrasse where members of the Gutmann family lived. Source: Google Maps; Michael S. Phillips Archive.

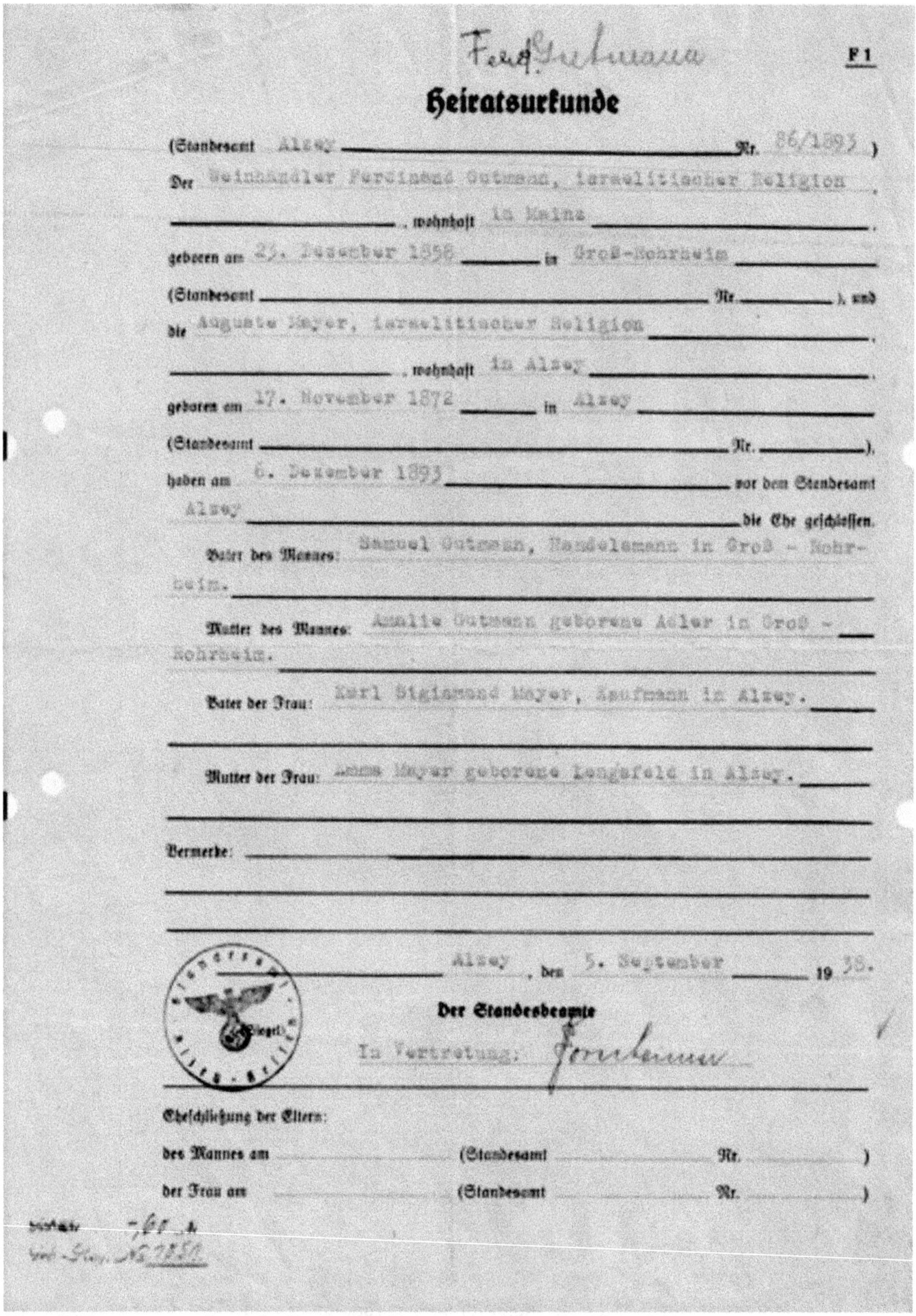

Feil Gutmann   **F 1**

Heiratsurkunde

(Standesamt Alzey _____ Nr. 86/1893)

Der Weinhändler Ferdinand Gutmann, israelitischer Religion

_____ wohnhaft in Mainz _____,

geboren am 23. Dezember 1856 _____ in Groß-Rohrheim _____

(Standesamt _____ Nr. _____), und

die Auguste Mayer, israelitischer Religion _____,

_____ wohnhaft in Alzey _____,

geboren am 17. November 1872 _____ in Alzey _____

(Standesamt _____ Nr. _____),

haben am 6. Dezember 1893 _____ vor dem Standesamt

Alzey _____ die Ehe geschlossen.

Vater des Mannes: Samuel Gutmann, Handelsmann in Groß – Rohr-

heim. _____

Mutter des Mannes: Amalie Gutmann geborene Adler in Groß –

Rohrheim. _____

Vater der Frau: Karl Sigismund Mayer, Kaufmann in Alzey. _____

_____

Mutter der Frau: Anna Mayer geborene Lengsfeld in Alzey. _____

_____

Vermerke: _____

_____

_____

Alzey , den 5. September _____ 19 38.

Der Standesbeamte

In Vertretung: *Fernbenner*

Eheschließung der Eltern:

des Mannes am _____ (Standesamt _____ Nr. _____)

der Frau am _____ (Standesamt _____ Nr. _____)

Fig. 1.7 Marriage certificate for Ferdinand Gutmann and Auguste 'Gustel' Mayer.
Auguste (my great grandmother) took over the family wine business upon her husband's death
on 15 August 1910. Source: Michael S. Phillips Archive.

Fig. 1.8 Auguste Gutmann. Source: Michael S. Phillips Archive.

Fig. 1.9 Auguste Gutmann.
My great-grandmother bundled up in her
furs standing on a frozen river Rhine.
Source: Michael S. Phillips Archive.

Fig. 1.10 My grandmother Milly (Amalie) Gutmann, her brother Karl and her sister Anna.
Source: Michael S. Phillips Archive.

Amalie (Milly) Schwarz
geborene Gutmann

geboren 1894 in Mainz
gestorben 1977 in Guildford, England

Anna Gutman

geboren 1900 in Mainz
ermordet 1942/45 in Riga oder Auschwitz

Fotos: Privatbesitz M. Philips

Das Mainzer Weinhändlerehepaar Ferdinand Gutmann (geboren 1858 in Groß-Rohrheim, gestorben 1910 in Mainz) und Auguste, geborene Mayer (geboren 1872 in Alzey, ermordet 1942/45 in Riga oder Auschwitz) hatte drei Kinder: Karl Max (geboren 1897, umgekommen in einem sowjetischen Lager 1945/46); Amalie und Anna.
Amalie besuchte die Höhere Töchterschule (Frauenlob-Gymnasium) von 1903 bis 1911, Anna von 1907 bis 1917.

Amalie heiratete 1920 den Fabrikbesitzer Walter Schwarz aus Greiz in Thüringen. Nach dem Tod ihres Mannes 1925 ließ sie sich mit den in Greiz geborenen Kindern Anneliese und Walter in Berlin nieder. Die Firma musste in der NS-Zeit zwangsweise veräußert, »arisiert« werden. Die Flucht aus Deutschland zusammen mit den Kindern gelang zu Beginn des Zweiten Weltkriegs. Die Tochter heiratete und lebte bis zu ihrem frühen Tod in England. Der Sohn wurde Arzt und wanderte nach dem Krieg mit der Familie nach Kanada aus.

Nach England wurde Amalie Schwarz von ihrer Schwester Anna Gutmann und der Mutter begleitet. Da für diese beiden dort niemand eine finanzielle Bürgschaft übernahm, reisten sie weiter nach Riga, wo der Bruder Karl Gutmann einen Zweig des Familienbetriebes leitete. Hier wähnten sie sich möglicherweise sicher. Es sollte jedoch anders kommen. Nach dem deutschen Überfall auf die Sowjetunion kam es auch zur Besetzung der bisher in sowjetischer Hand befindlichen baltischen Staaten.
Anna und ihre Mutter Auguste wurden irgendwann zwischen 1942 und 1945 in Riga selbst oder in Auschwitz Mordopfer des nazistischen Rassenwahns. Ebenso erging es Schwiegertochter Sonja Gutmann, geborene Herzfelder, und ihrem Sohn Joe Ferdinand. Karl Gutmann musste vermutlich an der russischen Front für die deutschen Angreifer Zwangsarbeit leisten, geriet in Gefangenschaft und starb 1945 oder 1946 in einem sowjetischen Zwangsarbeitslager.

RF
(Blick auf Mainzer Frauengeschichte 2005)

Fig. 1.11 Milly and Anna Remembered. Milly and her sister Anna feature in a Mainz women's calendar. Source: Frauenleben in Magenza, 2015.

Fig. 1.12 Milly Gutmann. This photo was taken when my grandmother was around 18 years old and eight years before she married Walter Schwarz in 1920. Source: Michael S. Phillips Archive.

Fig. 1.13 Berthe Goetz (née Weinmann).
Berthe and Milly were friends from the time they
were both young women. I believe Berthe, who
was older, was instrumental in introducing Milly
to her husband-to-be Walter Schwarz.
Source: Michael S. Phillips Archive.

Fig. 1.14 Walter Schwarz Silhouette Card.
Walter sent this card to my grandmother Milly,
his future wife, from Salzburg in July 1918. On
the reverse he wrote a love note in Old German.
Source: Michael S. Phillips Archive.

Fig. 1.15 Wedding of Walter Schwarz and Milly Gutmann, 11 May
1920. This picture of Milly in her wedding gown and Walter in
morning dress was probably taken inside 32 Kaiserstrasse.
Source: Michael S. Phillips Archive.

Fig. 1.16 Walter and Milly Schwarz (née Gutmann). Source: Michael S. Phillips Archive.

Fig. 1.17 Outside 32 Kaiserstrasse, 1936. Milly's children Anneliese (my mother) and Max Walter stand in the centre of the group on the pavement outside their grandmother Auguste's house. Source: Michael S. Phillips Archive.

Fig. 1.18 Karl and Sonja Gutmann (née Herzfeld). From the mid-1930s, Milly's brother Karl Gutmann worked for the Schwarz textile operation in Riga, Latvia, where he married Sonja Herzfeld in 1936. She gave birth to their son Joe in 1937. In 1939, Milly's mother Auguste and her sister Anna Gutmann joined the growing community of German exiles there, believing they would be safe. Source: Michael S. Phillips Archive.

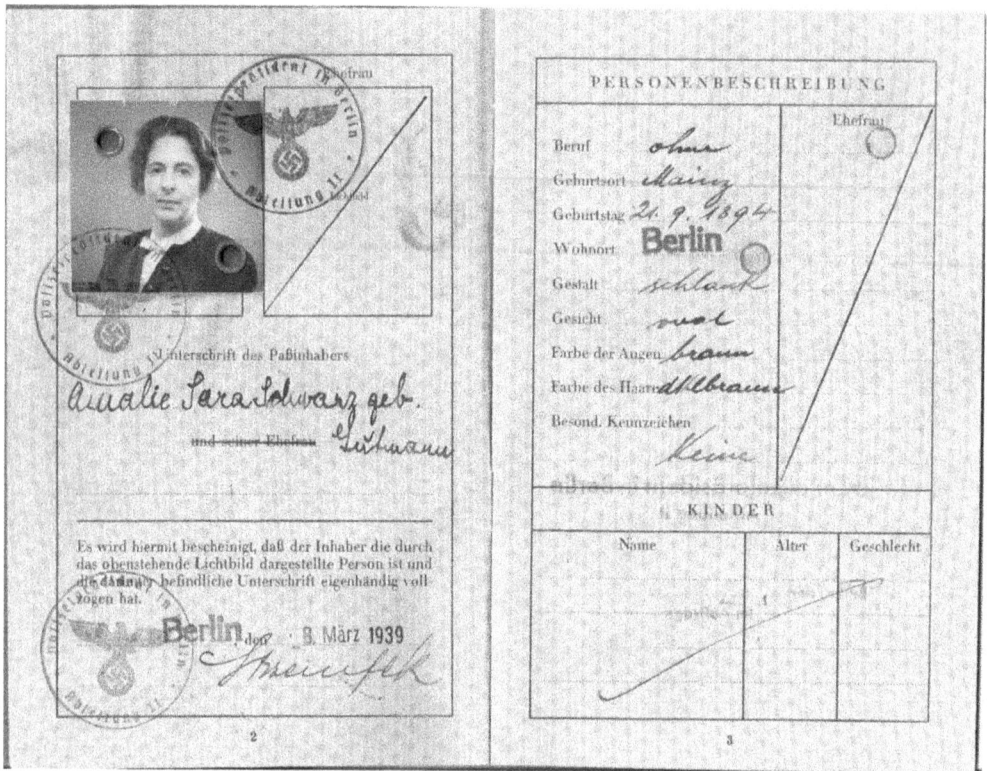

Fig. 1.19 Milly's Passport. Issued in Berlin, March 1939. Source: Michael S. Phillips Archive.

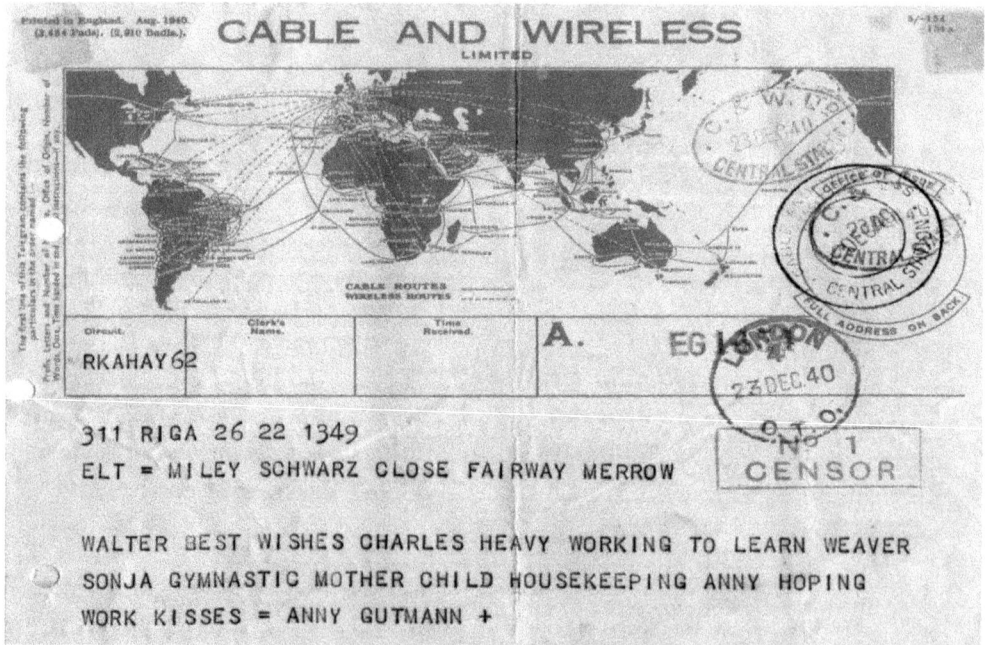

Fig. 1.20 Sent just before Christmas in 1940 and six months prior to the German invasion of Latvia, this telegram from Riga is the last communication my grandmother ever received from her sister Anna. Source: Michael S. Phillips Archive.

YAD VASHEM

The Holocaust Martyrs' and Heroes' Remembrance Authority
Hall of Names - P.O.B. 3477, Jerusalem 91034

יד ושם

רשות הזיכרון לשואה ולגבורה
היכל השמות - ת.ד 3477, ירושלים 91034

Page of Testimony דַּף עֵד

54612

Page of Testimony for commemoration of the Jews who perished during the Holocaust;
please fill in a separate form for each victim, in block capitals

The Martyrs' and Heroes' Remembrance Law 5713-1953 determines in section 2 that: "The task of Yad Vashem is
to gather into the homeland material regarding all those members of the Jewish people who laid down their
lives, who fought and rebelled against the Nazi enemy and his collaborators, and to perpetuate their names
and those of the communities, organizations and institutions which were destroyed because they were Jewish."

Victim's photo

Victim's family name:	Maiden name:
Gutmann	Mayer

Victim's first name (also nickname):	Previous/other family name:
Auguste, Sara	

Title:	Gender: FEMALE	Date of birth: November 1872 17	Approx. age at death: 70

Town of birth: Alzey	Region:	Country: GERMANY	Citizenship: GERMANY

Victim's father	First name: Karl, Sigismund	Family name: Mayer

Victim's mother	First name: Emma	Maiden name: Lengsfeld

Victim's wife/husband	First name: Ferdinand	Maiden name:	Victim's family status: WIDOW	Number of children: 3

Town of permanent residence: Mainz	Region:	Country: GERMANY	Street:

Profession: HOUSEWIFE	Place of work:	Member of organization/movement:

Place of residence during the war: Riga	Region:	Country: LATVIA	Street: Ghetto

Places, events and activities during the war (prison/deportation/ghetto/camp/ death march/hiding/escape/resistance/combat):

Place of death:	Region:	Country:	Date of death:

Circumstances of death:
unknown

I, the undersigned, hereby declare that this testimony is correct to the best of my knowledge.
I understand that this Page of Testimony and all the information on it will be publicly accessible.

First name: Ulrich	Family name: Dr. Bollert	Previous/maiden name:

Street: Ahornstraße 9	City: Bexbach	State/Zip code: 66450

Country: GERMANY	Shoah survivor: No	Relationship to victim (family/other): FAMILY FRIEND

Date: 12-11-2010	Place: Bexbach	Signature:

Ulrich I . Bollert

"וּנְתַתִּי לָהֶם בְּבֵיתִי וּבְחוֹמֹתַי יָד וָשֵׁם...אֲשֶׁר לֹא יִכָּרֵת" ישעיהו נ"ו ה
"And I shall give them in My house and within My walls a memorial and a name...that shall not be cut off" Isaiah 56:5

Fig. 1.21 Page of Testimony for Auguste Gutmann
These documents filed by friends and relatives of victims of the Holocaust are held by Yad Vashem
and are intended to restore the identities of those murdered and commemorate their lives, as well as
stand as a symbolic tombstone. Source: Yad Vashem, Hall of Names.

Fig. 1.22 32 Kaiserstrasse in 2018. Allied aerial bombing of Mainz in 1942 destroyed many of the buildings on Kaiserstrasse, including my grandmother's childhood home at 32 Kaiserstrasse. This office block now stands on the site. Photo by Nixnubix via Wikipedia.org.

Fig. 1.23 Milly Schwarz and Alice Morreau (née Weinmann). This picture was probably taken in the early '70s. Lifelong friends, Milly (left) and Alice (right), the sister of Berthe Goetz, sit in the sunshine drinking tea in (I believe) Alice's back garden in Guildford. Source: Michael S. Phillips Archive.

Chapter 2. The Jews of Mainz

During the Second World War, huge swathes of Mainz were levelled or set ablaze during heavy bombing by the British Royal Air Force and the US Air Force in raids that targeted the city in earnest from August 1942.[10] Sitting on the left bank of the Rhine River, only 120 or so kilometres from the modern-day border with France, the river port city's many medieval buildings were damaged or destroyed during the war. Some still stand, concentrated around the cobble-stoned market square and the 1,000-year old Roman Catholic St Martin's Cathedral.

The buildings on Kaiserstrasse, four and five-storey mansions facing onto a central park planted with trees, flowerbeds and lawns, splendid late 19th century properties adorned with pillars and porticos, domes, mansard roofs and elaborate cornicing cherry-picked from neo-classical, baroque, renaissance or art deco designs, were also badly damaged or completely destroyed during Allied bombing. Of the houses that still stand today, many are now protected cultural monuments.

The building in Petersstrasse where my grandmother and her sister attended school was also destroyed. The Höhere Mädchenschule (higher girls' school) was founded in 1889. In 1938 it was renamed Frauenlobschule after the medieval lyricist and minstrel Heinrich von Meissen, known as Frauenlob, who died in Mainz in 1318 and is buried in the cloister of the cathedral. After the war, the school was moved to its new location in Adam-Karrillon-Strasse, where it remains to this day. Today's Frauenlob-Gymnasium has male and female pupils. Its earlier importance as the place where many Jewish girls were educated is not obvious. There are only about 1,100 Jews currently living in Mainz out of a population of around 220,000.[11]

Mainz, now the capital of the federal state of Rhineland-Palat-
inate (Rheinland-Pfalz) in southwest Germany, has served as an
important cultural centre for Christians and Jews. Johannes Gutenberg, who invented printing with movable type and the printing
press that revolutionised the production of printed books and published the Gutenberg Bible, lived in Mainz in the 15th century. Less
well known is the depth of Jewish history.

By the advent of the Nazi regime, Jews had been living in the area
for more than 1,000 years.[12] In fact, the Jewish community in Mainz
was among the earliest documented living in central and Eastern
Europe. With the nearby towns of Worms and Speyer, Mainz was a
centre of rabbinical learning and Jewish life dating back to the 11th
century.[13] Jews also lived in Frankfurt, just over 40 kilometres east,
close by Darmstadt, and Wiesbaden to the north of Mainz. Jewish
scholars from the Rhineland had a unique influence on the develop-
ment of Ashkenazi Judaism passing down legal decisions, traditions,
rights and customs still adhered to today.[14] Among notable thinkers,
Rabbi Gershom ben Judah (c. 960-1040), referred to as the Light of
Exile and widely attributed to have authored among many significant edicts the Jewish ban on polygamy, lived in Mainz.[15]

Rabenu Solomon Yitzchaki (1040-1105), a Talmudic commen-
tator from Troyes in France, better known as Rashi, also studied
and taught in Worms and Mainz.[16] He was instrumental in shaping
rabbinical traditions of learning and his commentaries, notable for
their clarity, are still in universal use today. (He also made a living
selling wine).

The Old Jewish cemetery (known as the Judensand) on Mombacher Strasse—previously home to the oldest Jewish gravestone
in central Europe, inscribed with the date 1049 (it nows sits in the
Landesmuseum)—literally sets this legacy in stone. Over time, the

cemetery has been subject to desecration, damage and the removal of some of its headstones to use as masonry. However it still served as a burial ground until 1880 when the New Jewish Cemetery was opened on Untere Zahlbacher Strasse, next to the Mainz Central Cemetery. My grandmother's father Ferdinand and his cousin Max Gutmann and his wife Rosalie are all buried there.

I mention this history not because my grandmother's family were at all observant—that ended with earlier generations—but to highlight the reach of Jewish roots in the area.

One of the most significant members of the Mainz Jewish community for the purposes of my research was Michel Oppenheim, a well-known local figure who compiled the Oppenheim Lists.[17] Born in 1885, Michel was the son of Ludwig Oppenheim, a Jewish lawyer from Mainz, and Elise Hopf, a Catholic from Nuremberg. The family lived at 94 Kaiserstrasse. Michel married Erna von Zakrzewski, a Catholic, in 1921 and they had their only child Ludwig a year later.

After a career as a lawyer, a soldier for the duration of the First World War, and a civil servant at the Mainz District of the Provisional Directorate Rheinhessen, where Michel was appointed to the Government Council responsible for matters related to the French occupation, he was forced to retire in 1934 for "racial reasons" outlined in the Nazi Law for the Restoration of the Civil Service. Around the same time, he and his wife sent their son to Switzerland for his own safety.[18]

In March 1941, Oppenheim was forced to act as liaison between the Gestapo and the Reich Association of Jews in Germany, a Jewish organisation co-opted in 1939 to administer the elimination of the Jewish community and "Gentiles of Jewish Descent" in Germany.[19] Its Special Referee for the Affairs of the Jews was Adolf Eichmann.

All individuals deemed Jewish by the Nazi regime (i.e. anyone of Jewish descent or faith; Gentiles with three or four Jewish grandparents; anyone with two Jewish grandparents who was married to a Jew) were forced to join the organisation, contribute fees to pay for its administration and wear a yellow star.

As regular deportations of German Jews accelerated in October 1941 to newly occupied countries in the east, Oppenheim's gruesome task was to draw up deportation lists, which he detailed in a secret journal. I have relied heavily on these lists in my research.

Residents of Kaiserstrasse appear on the Oppenheim Lists, although it is unlikely he documented everyone who fled, hid or were murdered. In my research, I discovered that more than a few of the older Jewish residents of Kaiserstrasse committed suicide prior to deportation, or they died in the Jewish hospital, probably helped along by the medical staff there. The timing of their deaths suggests they had prior knowledge they were listed on an upcoming transport. I suspect Oppenheim warned individuals of their pending fate, but I have no way of proving that. Unlike many Jews forced to work for the Nazis, Oppenheim survived the war and became a city official, helping spearhead the revival of the arts and the city's cultural life and that of the university. He died in 1963.

Kaiserstrasse

My grandmother, who viewed herself as German, was born into a highly assimilated but tight-knit community that lived in close proximity to one another. I attribute the concentration of Jewish families on Kaiserstrasse and the surrounding streets to their wealth and the interrelatedness of those particular families and their commercial ties.

Max Gutmann would have bought 32 Kaiserstrasse not long after it was built. Conceived as a boulevard, the street was constructed in the late 19th century as part of the city's much needed expansion. Named after Kaiser Wilhelm I, and running for about a kilometre from the main train station at its south west end to the magnificently domed Protestant Christuskirche (completed in 1903) and the Rhine in the north east, it was intended to be a central thoroughfare connecting the old town with the new city (Neustadt) spreading out to the west. It remains a critical transportation route.

Although the house at 32 Kaiserstrasse where my grandmother lived was destroyed, the street holds unique importance to me as a place she loved. A modern feature is the number of stolpersteine, so-called 'stumbling stones', embedded in the pavement.[20] The small concrete bricks overlaid with brass serve as individual memorials to Jewish persons or families persecuted and exterminated by the Nazi regime. Each brass plaque is engraved with a name and dates of birth, deportation, death or escape—if known—and marks the individual's last residence of choice. There are three individual plaques outside number 32 commemorating my grandmother's mother Auguste, her sister Anna, and brother Karl.

Fig. 2.1   14 Kaiserstrasse: The house as it was in the early twentieth century. Source: Mainz City Archives, Reference BPSF/20389 A..

Fig. 2.2 21 Kaiserstrasse. As of 1939 Nazi legislation ensured that Jews were no longer allowed to be property owners. Their houses were taken and often used as so-called 'judenhäuser' where members of the Jewish community from Mainz and surrounding villages were detained in crowded accommodations prior to deportation. The house had belonged to lawyer Paul Simon, who emigrated to the US in 1938 with his family. One of his tenants was Michel Oppenheim. Source: Mainz City Archives, Reference BPSF1893 A.

Fig. 2.3 28 Kaiserstrasse. Along with numbers 26 and 30, this building was home to the H. Sichel Söhne wine business and the extended Sichel family that ran it. Public domain, source: Unknown.

Fig. 2.4 35 Kaiserstrasse. Source: Mainz
City Archives, Reference: BPSF/1547 B.

Fig. 2.5 71 Kaiserstrasse. Public domain. Source:
Wikipedia.org.

Fig. 2.6 Kaiserstrasse. Source: Mainz City Archives, Reference: BPSF/20386 A.

Fig. 2.7 50 Kaiserstrasse (building in the middle), September 1899 postcard. Source: Mainz City Archives, Reference: BPSF/1892 A.

Fig. 2.8 52 Kaiserstrasse in 2007. Photographer: Symposiarch, via Wikipedia.org.

Fig. 2.9 80/82 Kaiserstrasse. Source: Mainz City Archives, Reference BPSF: 20387 A

Fig. 2.10 Christuskirche. Completed in 1903, the huge Protestant church stands at the northeast end of the street close to the Rhine. Public domain.via:Wikipedia.org.

Fig. 2.11 Looking Northeast toward the Rhine, from postcard, c.1908. Public domain.

Fig. 2.12 Höhere Mädchenschule, Petersstrasse, Mainz, 1929. The high school for girls Milly and Anna and many of their friends, family members and neighbours attended. Source: Mainzer Frauengeschichte. Courtesy of Mainz City Archives, Reference: BPSK/654.

Fig. 2.13 Frauenlob-Gymnasium, Adam-Karrillon-Strasse, Mainz, 2018
After 1945, the former boys' school became the new location of the Höhere
Mädchenschule. It is now a mixed school. Source: Michael S. Phillips Archive.

Fig. 2.14 53 Kaiserstrasse in 2018. The plot was redeveloped following Allied
bombing during the war. Photo by Nixnubix via Wikipedia.org.

Fig. 2.15 61 Kaiserstrasse.
The house next door at No. 59
has been rebuilt but would have
originally been constructed in the
same style. Source: Michael S.
Phillips Archive.

Fig. 2.16 Michel Oppenheim.
A trained lawyer, First World War veteran
and former civil servant, Oppenheim
was appointed as a liaison between
the Gestapo and the Mainz Jewish
community. His deportation lists, with
copies compiled in secret, detailed
the fate of its members and form the
backbone of my research.
Source: Genealogy.com, courtesy of
Richard G. Simon.

Chapter 3. Persecution

The history of Jews in Mainz (and elsewhere in Germany and Europe) is punctuated with anti-Semitic attacks, forced conversions, the imposition of special taxes, violence and murder. In the 11th and 12th centuries Jewish people suffered Crusaders' assaults, pogroms in the 13th century, expulsions in the 15th, and additional sanctions and restrictions under French rule in the 17th century.[21] Conversely, the occupation of Mainz at the end of the 18th century by French revolutionary troops brought with it freedoms for the Jewish community. Jews were allowed to open their own schools and the gates of the ghetto were removed.[22] Mainz, as the capital of the Département du Mont Tonnerre, belonged to France from 1798 to 1814. The civil code decreed by Napoleon in 1804 finally granted equal civic status to the Jews of Mainz.[23]

The rise of the Nazi movement in the 1920s and the actions of the regime throughout the 1930s reversed the assimilation of German Jews. It impacted the Jewish residents of Kaiserstrasse in many ways. At a superficial level, the first section of the street, numbers 1-15 and 2-20 on the other side, was renamed Horst-Wessel-Platz after a mythologised leader of a Berlin section of the Sturmabteilung, the Nazi storm troopers, (a brown-shirted mob deployed to harass, intimidate and attack opponents). After Wessel's murder in 1930, Joseph Goebbels elevated him to a so-called Nazi martyr.

In 1933, the new Chancellor Adolf Hitler declared a boycott of Jewish-owned businesses, dealing a devastating blow to the economic health and social status of Jewish families.[24] The Nuremberg race laws were decreed September 1935 and implemented the following summer. Among provisions, the legislation stripped Jews of their right to citizenship and the protections that carried, and banned Jews and non-Jews from marrying.[25] The pogroms of Kristallnacht on 9-10 November 1938 carried out by paramilitaries and local mobs, the failure of the local authorities to intervene, and the arrest of Jewish men that followed, ramped up the persecution of Jews across Germany.[26]

For some Jewish residents of Kaiserstrasse, like my grandmother's mother Auguste and sister Anny, the writing was on the wall. (Brother Karl had already left in 1933 for Riga). By the time the Second World War began, the number of Jewish residents in Mainz had dwindled to around 1,500 from 2,730 in 1933.[27]

At the Wannsee Conference on 20 January 1942, where senior Nazi government officials and the SS leadership consolidated plans—already in motion—to rid Germany and Nazi-occupied Europe of its Jewish population through mass deportation and extermination, SS-Obergruppenführer Reinhard Heydrich reported that between 1933 and October 1941 more than half a million German, Austrian and Czech Jews had emigrated.[28] Those that were left were subjected to systematic murder.[29]

Writing with the benefit of hindsight, some of Kaiserstrasse's Jewish residents missed their chance to escape by a hair's breadth. Some were too old, lacked funds, or exit permits, or were perhaps in denial about just how murderous the persecution of Jews had become and refused to leave their homes. Others were betrayed by those they should have been able to trust.

Carl Theodor Frank, a wealthy timber merchant, who owned 94 Kaiserstrasse,[30] (where his stolperstein is laid) was born in Worms in 1858. He was an old man when the war began. His wife Mathilde had died in 1933 and his three children, William Gustav (b. 1885), Rudolf (b. 1886), and Hildegard Martha (b. 1901) had fled Germany. William Frank, a doctor, settled in the US with his family. Rudolf survived in Switzerland, while his daughter and her husband were registered living in London in the 1960s. Frank lived alone in an apartment occupying the first floor of the house. The other floors of the building had been converted into flats and rented out to tenants. With an eye to purchasing the building at a discounted price, after Kristallnacht, one of his tenants informed the Gestapo that Carl was Jewish. Carl remained living in his flat—presumably paying rent—for some time. Finally he was forced to move to 25 Breidenbacherstrasse, a crowded home for elderly Jews. From there, blind and in his eighties, he was deported to Theresienstadt, a transit camp-ghetto in northwest Czechoslovakia.[31]

Many Kaiserstrasse residents experienced the deprivations of Theresienstadt.[32] The camp opened in November 1941 as a detention centre for Czech Jews pending deportation to forced-labour or concentration camps elsewhere in Nazi-occupied Europe. It also held Austrian, Czech and German Jews, who were selected on the basis of their age, past military service and how well they were known in the arts and cultural life of their countries of origin.[33] Given the talents of the detainees, the camp had a rich cultural scene. The regime presented the camp as a model of Jewish life under the Third Reich, lying to the international community to obscure the reality of disease, overcrowding and malnutrition. Carl starved to death in an attic room.[34]

The Ladenburg Brothers

Others missed their escape by cruel interference. The Ladenburg brothers were such a case, according to research conducted by Renate Knigge-Tesche.[35] Karl Moritz Ladenburg (b. 1895) and his brother Siegfried Ladenburg (b. 1899) grew up on Kaiserstrasse. Their father, Zacharias Ladenburg (1845-1933) was a real estate and mortgage broker, who had inherited his business, Moritz Ladenburg & Son, from his father.[36] Zacharias and his wife Flora and their two sons must have been among the first families to live on Kaiserstrasse, occupying number 11 from 1894. For a while before the First World War, the business was based out of 18 Kaiserstrasse before it moved to number 11 and remained there.

The boys' mother died when they were young children (seven and three) and their father brought them up.[37] Both fought in the First World War and Karl was awarded the Hessian Medal for Bravery. In the 1920s, they joined their father in business.

Karl, a qualified lawyer who did not practise, was active in local Jewish life, and one of the founders of the Association for the Care of Jewish Antiquities, which in 1925 contributed exhibits to the Jewish section of the Millennium Exhibition on Rhineland-German Culture, according to Knigge-Tesche.[38]

A year later, the association founded the Museum of Jewish Antiquities in an annexe of the new synagogue that opened in 1912 on Hindenburgstrasse, a main street perpendicular to Kaiserstrasse, running west.

Upon their father's death in 1933, the Ladenburg brothers took ownership of the business.[39] It was not a propitious time. To a regime set on appropriating Jewish property, including houses and precious goods, as well as businesses and bank accounts, the Ladenburg brothers would have been tempting targets for a kleptocratic regime.

After Kristallnacht, from 11 November until 17 December 1938, Karl was arrested and held in Buchenwald concentration camp. After his release, both brothers were kept under surveillance. They were detained a year later from 11 August to 4 November for alleged "foreign exchange offences". They were not convicted but they were subject to a security order that denied them free access to their bank accounts. They had to apply for expenses, including the money to emigrate. It was not granted.[40]

In April 1941, Karl and Siegfried were forced to sell 11 Kaiserstrasse to raise the finances for their journey. However, the Reich retained the funds and instead they were compelled to apply again for money to pay rent on the property they formerly owned.[41] They were forcibly moved a year later to 58 Adam-Karrillon-Strasse (parallel to Kaiserstrasse), to a formerly Jewish-owned property that had been commandeered as a so-called judenhaus,[42] a building where Jews were rehoused, isolated from the broader community, and often under curfew. These houses evolved from mini-ghettos, which segregated Jews from 'Aryans', to staging posts prior to deportation to the death camps. The brothers shared a room together, and a kitchen with eight other people.

In March 1942 they tried to flee, having unofficially learned that they were on the list for the 25 March transport to Piaski. They were arrested in Cologne, however. Both were taken to Frankfurt police prison and put under 'protective custody' (Schutzhaft) by the Darmstadt Gestapo. While they were detained, their room in the judenhaus was cleared, writes Knigge-Tesche. Her research has a predictably wretched conclusion. In July, the brothers were transferred to Buchenwald concentration camp, where Siegfried was shot weeks later, allegedly trying to escape, and Karl died in October of 'flu'(!), according to records. Their graves can be found in the New Jewish Cemetery.[43]

The Haas Family

For Alfred Haas, born in Mainz in 1892, and his family, time ran out. An internist and specialist in nervous conditions, Alfred's medical

licence (issued in 1917) was revoked in 1938. Since 1933, Jewish people of all ages and in all professions had been subject to increasingly
punitive anti-Jewish legislation, including limiting the number of
Jewish pupils in public schools prior to their outright expulsion in
1938; excluding Jewish administrators from the civil service; pre-
venting Jews from approaching the bar; and banning Jews from
editorial positions and working as tax accountants, veterinarians,
public school teachers and midwives and from serving in the army.
Indicative of the invasive scrutiny and arbitrary cruelty the community endured, by the end of 1938, Jews were banned even from
owning carrier pigeons.[44]

In October of the same year, the Reich government issued legislation requiring Jews to hand in their passports to be stamped with
the letter 'J' or be rendered invalid. A month later, the Reich official-
ly closed all Jewish owned businesses and passed new laws to restrict
the movement of Jews.[45]

In 1938, Alfred sought transit visas from the Belgium Consulate
in Cologne for himself and his wife Irma (b. 1911) with the goal of
emigrating to the US via Belgium. They did not make it out. In July
1939, Alfred and Irma had a son Gerson. They were still living at
their family home at 20 Kaiserstrasse where Dr. Haas also had his
medical practice. By 1941, they had been moved to 21 Kaiserstrasse,
a judenhaus. They were allocated two rooms and shared a kitchen
with Berthe and Jenny Schönberger and Berthe Bamberger, who
were all to commit suicide in the face of deportation. A year later,
the Haas family was moved to the Jewish home for the elderly on
Gonsenheimer Strasse, most likely because Dr. Haas suffered from
multiple sclerosis and could hardly walk. Such places served as gath-
ering points prior to deportation. Alfred was 50 years old, his wife
was 33, and their son just three. From there the family was taken to

Theresienstadt. Alfred was dead by the end of the year. Irma and Gerson managed to survive for a further 18 months before they were killed at Auschwitz.

Irma's parents, Louis and Johanna Hartogs, did succeed in obtaining a temporary Belgian residency permit and fled to Borgerhout near Antwerp en route to the US. However, the German invasion of Belgium in May 1940 put an end to their plans. They moved locations twice, to Antwerp and then to Kwaadmechelen, before they were detained and sent in September 1942 to Mechelen transit camp in Belgium. The camp was established in a former barracks. For the Nazis, Mechelen was ideally situated between Antwerp and Brussels, two cities with sizeable Jewish populations, and offered good rail connections.[46] From there, Louis and Johanna were deported to Auschwitz where they were murdered. He was 72; she was 57. Rather than a place of sanctuary, Belgium had been a trap.

Their son Renatus (b. 1909 in Mainz), Irma's brother, was luckier. He had studied medicine in Brussels, practised in Belgium and married a Belgian woman from Antwerp, Nelly Gutwirth. They escaped to Lisbon via Bordeaux where the Portuguese consul issued them an entry visa. From Portugal, they travelled to the US, where he was to become a psychologist. He died in 1998.

Missed Chances

Another Kaiserstrasse resident, Hildegard Heymann (b. 1904), who lived at number 29, had a relative in the US who was prepared to pay for her travel costs. It was too late, however, for her to take advantage of this help. The Nazi regime closed the doors on Jewish emigration in October 1941. According to the Mainz deportation lists and the German Gedenkbuch, Hildegard was taken with around 1,000 Jews from Southern Hesse, including 470 from Mainz, loaded on to train Da 14 on 25 March 1942 at Darmstadt—the main deportation assembly point for this transport—and sent to the Piaski ghetto in German-occupied Poland.[47]

According to the Yad Vashem archives, in Mainz, Jewish deportees were rounded up from either the judenhaus where they had been detained, or brought from their houses or nearby towns, to the Feldberg School gym and then onto the freight station at Mombacher Strasse. The deportation ramp stood a few hundred metres from the main station at the top of Kaiserstrasse and opposite the Old Jewish Cemetery. They were required to bring with them 50 Reichsmarks, a suitcase, and a set of clothes, food for two weeks, bedding and tableware, and a list of their assets.[48] Their identification papers were taken and they were forced to wear a cardboard sign around their neck showing their name, date of birth and deportation number as they were shunted up the ramp. Upon arrival in Poland at Trawniki train station days later, they were marched 12 kilometres to Piaski where they took over accommodation vacated by local Jews who had been sent to Belzec extermination camp.[49]

Hildegard died in Piaski in December 1942. The ghetto was liquidated the following spring. In a grim example of the mechanics of Nazi bureaucracy, the relative who had paid for her passage was refunded their money.

Maximilian Franz Carlebach (b. 1883 and known as Franz), a Mainz lawyer, also just missed his chance. He lived at 31 Kaiserstrasse, a handsome redbrick, five-storey building on a corner in the middle of the street, which was commandeered as Gestapo headquarters. According to documents dated 1934, the building was owned by the Goldschmidt family and divided into four flats.

Franz's first cousin Herbert Carlebach lived in New York and paid for Franz's passage to the US, but it was too late. By then, it is likely that Franz was already detained in the Sachsenhausen concentration camp near Berlin, where he died in March 1942.

Franz had converted to Christianity in 1906, but this made no difference under the fastidious implementation of the Law for the Protection of German Blood and Honour, passed in 1935, that detailed who was eligible for Reich citizenship.[50] The law established convoluted criteria for determining an individual's race under the categories of 'German-blooded', first degree mixed race ('mischlinge'), second degree mixed race, and Jew.[51] The regime returned Herbert's money in 1944.

The Mayers

Bernhard Albert Mayer (b. 1866), arguably one of the most prominent members of the Jewish community prior to the Second World War, and his wife Adele Deborah (b. 1873, née Trier) escaped by the skin of their teeth. They lived at number 49 and are one of many Mayer families with a connection to Kaiserstrasse. Other members of the family lived at number 53, where the family business was based.

Mayer was a very common Jewish surname in Mainz before the war and can be traced back to Martin Mayer, who was born in Ichenhausen in 1762 and arrived in Mainz in 1794 where he married Rosalie Coma. Martin and Rosalie were the grandparents of Rosalie Gutmann (née Mayer), the wife of Max Gutmann, the founder of the Max Gutmann wine merchants of 32 Kaiserstrasse.

Bernhard Albert was descended from a different strand. From Dr. Hedwig Brüchert's contribution to the book *Der Neue Jüdische Friedhof in Mainz*[52] (The New Jewish Cemetery in Mainz) I learned that Bernhard Albert's father Martin (b. 1838, and named after his grandfather) was key to raising the family's social and financial status and establishing their presence on Kaiserstrasse. Dr. Brüchert is responsible for unearthing much of the information that follows.

Prior to Martin's marriage to Rosalie Altschüler in 1865, he founded a jewellery business with his younger brother Bernard Albert.[53] The Martin Mayer workshops made luxury pieces of real silver often set with semi-precious stones. As the business expanded it established new factories, took on new investors and Martin's sons Bernhard Albert and Eduard became co-owners. The business moved premises at the end of the 19th century to 53 Kaiserstrasse, where Martin also lived. As it continued to grow, they set up a branch in Pforzheim, a city known for its jewellery and watchmaking.[54]

Martin also played an important role in the community's religious life. The Judaica collection of the Landesmuseum Mainz displays a Torah crown made of gilded silver that the Martin Mayer workshop produced and which was donated to his congregation in 1898.[55] A year after his brother Bernard Albert died (1903) Martin passed away and the business passed into the hands of Martin's son Bernhard Albert, who took charge with the support of his cousins Albert and Ernst, the sons of his uncle Bernard. His brother Eduard had died five years before.

Bernhard Albert lived at 49 Kaiserstrasse—just down the street from the business premises—with his wife Adele Debora from Darmstadt and their four children. In 1934, silver production moved entirely to Pforzheim, supervised by Bernhard Albert's youngest son Martin Wilhelm, who was 20 years old.[56]

Following in his father's footsteps, Bernhard Albert also played a prominent role in public life, serving on the Mainz City Council from 1911-1918 and again from 1926-1929, and was given the honorary title of 'Kommerzienrat' or councillor of commerce. He was also a leader of the Gesamtgemeinde, the Israelite Religious Community[57], an organisation that Brüchert says was set up to represent both Orthodox and Reform Jews as one community when dealing with the state, although the congregation had split in the 19th century and worshipped in different synagogues with different rabbis. In 1904, he was elected to the Community's executive committee and then as president in 1908, a position he held until he emigrated in 1941.[58]

During this time, Bernhard Albert would have enjoyed the privileges of a wealthy and well-respected Mainz businessman with connections to prominent local Jewish religious figures such as Rabbi Professor Sigmund Salfeld and his successor Rabbi Dr Sali Levi, a veteran of the First World War and an active participant in preserving Mainz's Jewish cultural heritage. He served as chairman of the Association for the Care of Jewish Antiquities in Mainz.

The opening in 1912 of the new main synagogue was a milestone for Reform Jews in Mainz. The beautiful domed building constructed on the corner of Hindenburgstrasse and Josefsstrasse comprised two wings, community rooms, a wedding hall and—from 1926—the Museum of Jewish Antiquities. It was intended to serve the needs of members of the liberal Jewish community who had left their historical quarter in the old city and moved west, as the city grew, to new accommodations. Its inauguration was a grand event attended by the leaders of the state and city authorities as well as the clergy. Signifying both his secular and religious influence, upon the opening, Bernhard Albert was awarded the Knight's Cross I Class of the Grand Ducal Hessian Order of Philip the Magnanimous.[59]

However, in the 1930s the synagogue took on a new role, providing space for the Jewish District School that moved in as Jewish children were excluded from public schools and it hosted a soup kitchen to feed the needy. When the synagogue was set on fire and precious sacred objects were looted during Kristallnacht, 72-year old Bernhard Albert and fellow members of the congregation suffered a blow (to say the least). The remains of this grand building were destroyed days later. The Orthodox synagogue on the corner of Vordere Synagogenstrasse and Margarethengasse in the centre of the old Jewish quarter, which had operated as a house of prayer since the 1850s, was also destroyed.

The Israelite Religious Community, which offered both spiritual and practical support to Jews during this increasingly dangerous time, moved into a house at 2 Horst-Wessel-Strasse arranging classrooms on the ground floor and a meeting room above where Rabbi Sali Levi continued to hold services.[60] The Community helped Mainz Jews navigate increasingly complex anti-Jewish bureaucracy, which carried fatal penalties for submitting incorrect information, and to simply survive. It established an office to issue food vouchers and clothes, and opened a shoe repair workshop.

In 1938, the county health department confiscated the medical equipment at the Jewish hospital, where Jewish doctors and nurses were permitted to treat Jewish patients exclusively. The facility evolved into a home for the elderly and sick. Another Jewish old people's home had been established at the former Scharff sanatorium in Mainz-Gonsenheim in the spring of 1939. Rather than comfortable places for residents to see out their days, these homes were to evolve into deportation centres.

In 1938, the Martin Mayer silverware operations in Pforzheim were appropriated by George Lauer AG.[61] Bernhard Albert and his wife Adele (who was a distant cousin of my great grandmother's) prepared to leave. By this time they are registered at number 53. Their eldest son Karl Jakob (b. 1894), who had taken on his maternal grandfather's iron wholesaler business, Gebrüder Trier in Darmstadt, before he emigrated to Argentina in 1938, arranged visas for his parents. In March 1941, they made their way to Berlin, the only place from which Jews were allowed to exit. I could not find records confirming their port of departure, but they sailed to safety in Buenos Aires.

They were the final members of their family to escape. Their second son Ernst Bernhard (b. 1896), who worked with his brother Karl, had emigrated with his family to the US. Prior to the start of the war, their daughter Elisabeth Dora (b. 1900) sent her two children to the UK on the Kindertransport,[62] and hid with her husband Hans Gebhardt in the Netherlands in various locations. Miraculously, they survived the war. Bernhard Albert and Adele's youngest son Martin Wilhelm fled to England in 1938, via the Netherlands.[63]

Adele died in Buenos Aires in 1945 aged 72, followed by her husband two years later. Bernhard Albert was 81. They were safe but exiled from a home where they had lived for most of their long lives.

Frohwein Brothers

The Jewish community in Mainz during the 1930s was changing size and shape as people left seeking sanctuary overseas, while others arrived from the countryside and surrounding area, deeming it safer to be part of a larger community, or were forced from their homes. Later, Jews from nearby towns and villages would be corralled into judenhäuser in Mainz pending deportation. Families too were in flux.

The Frohweins were a family of butchers from Hochheim, a town 15 kilometres from Mainz. By 1936, three of the brothers, Joseph Friedrich (b. 1893), known as Fritz, Siegbert, known as Siegfried (b. 1891) and Benjamin Walter (b. 1903), known as Walter, had moved to Mainz.

Their older brother Julius Jakob Zvi (b. 1890) had been killed in the First World War. Middle brother Jehuda Ludwig (b. 1887) and younger brother Ernst (b. 1906) appear to have remained in Hochheim before they left for the UK and settled with their father Salomon Frohwein (b. 1863) in London. Their mother Helene (1863-1927) was already dead. Ludwig died in London in 1942 followed by his father two years later.

In 1936, Walter left for Belgium and Friedrich for England, with his family. Their sister Eva (Chava) Hertha Kaufmann (b. 1895, née Frohwein) escaped to the US and lived in New York. She died in Cincinnati in December 1973. However, Friedrich and Siegfried were still registered at 12 Horst-Wessel-Platz (12 Kaiserstrasse) in 1938.

Siegfried fled Germany in 1941, sponsored by a relative, Hans Frohwein, who had made it to Bogotá in Colombia. Hans paid for Siegfried's passage and he left on the SS Tenerife in November 1941. His wife Erna (b. 1898, née Guggenheim) and their daughter Ellen (b. 1933) appear to have tried to escape via Belgium, where they were arrested and imprisoned at Mechelen transit camp near Antwerp before they were deported to Auschwitz in 1942 and murdered.

Siegfried joined his sister Herta in New York, where he was still living in 1950 when he applied to be naturalised. But he did not live out his days there. He died in 1971 in Ireland where he had moved to run a cattle business that supplied meat to his brothers Walter, Friedrich and Ernst who all continued to work as butchers in London. They died there in 1958, 1968, and 1996 respectively.

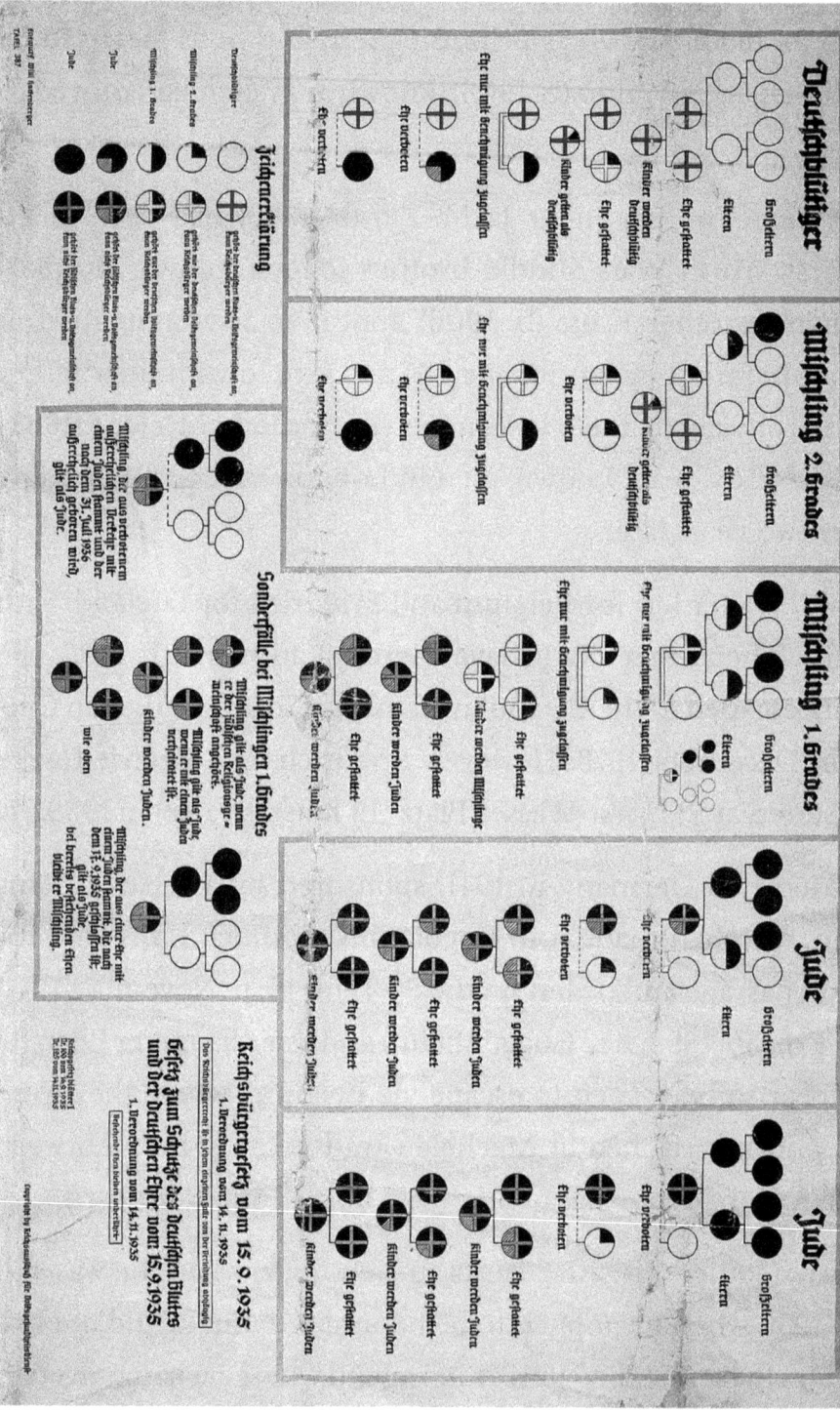

Fig. 3.1   Nuremberg Race Chart. The chart demonstrates the racial categories described in the Nuremberg laws passed in 1935. These classifications determined access to employment, finances, public transport and other public spaces, housing, rations, healthcare and ultimately a person's right to exist. Public domain. Source: Wikipedia.org.

Fig. 3.2 Carl Theodor Frank, c. 1900; sons Rudolf and William, c. 1894. Courtesy of Lisa Wasserman Weissberg.

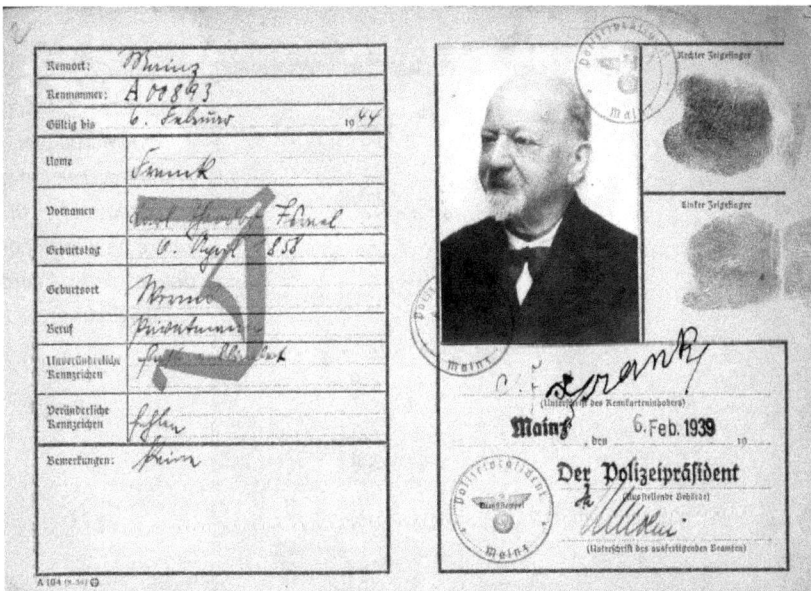

Fig. 3.3 Carl Theodor Frank Kennkarte. Kennkarten (civilian identity cards) were introduced in 1938. Those issued to Jews were printed on grey linen paper and marked by a red capital J. Source: Central Archive for the Study of the History of the Jews in Germany. The examples in this book are copies, most likely retained by the Mainz police, while the holder kept the original. How these cards managed to survive the war is unclear, and their existence is exceptional.

Fig. 3. 4. 94 Kaiserstrasse today (the original building was destroyed in the war)
Source: Michael S. Phillips Archive.

Fig. 3.5   Carl Theodor Frank
Stolperstein, 94 Kaiserstrassse.
The memorial plaque embedded
in the pavement notes Carl's
name, date of birth, when and
where he was deported and his
date of death. Source: Michael S.
Phillips Archive.

Fig. 3.6 Museum of Jewish Antiquities c. 1929. Source: GDKE RLP, Landesmuseum Mainz (U. Rudischer).

Fig. 3.7 Stolpersteine for Karl Moritz and Siegfried Ladenburg, 11 Kaiserstrasse. Photo by Nixnubix via:Wikipedia.org.

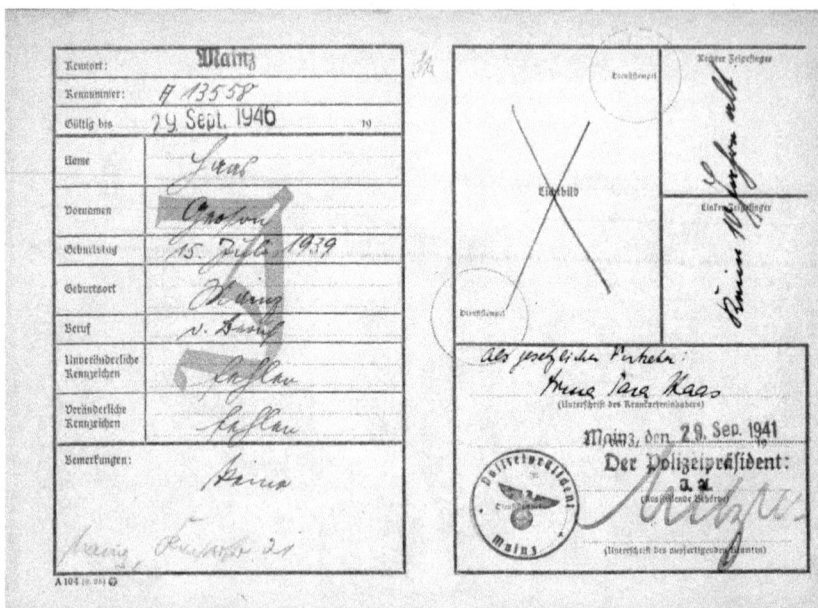

Fig. 3.8. Gerson Haas Kennkarte.
There is no picture of Gerson on the card, probably because he was only two when
it was issued. He was murdered at Auschwitz with his mother Irma (neé Hartogs).
She died in 1944. By then, the child's father Dr Alfred Haas was already dead. He
was murdered at Theresienstadt in 1942. Source: Central Archive for the Study of the
History of the Jews in Germany.

Fig. 3.9 Haas family stolpersteine, 20 Kaiserstrasse. Photo by Nixnubix via Wikipedia.org.

Fig. 3.10 20 Kaiserstrasse. This end of the street closest to the railway station was renamed Horst-Wessel-Platz in the 1930s after a Berlin leader of the Nazi Stormtroopers who was killed in 1930 and reimagined as a Nazi martyr. The original pre-war building was divided into flats and was the home of the Haas family. Dr. Alfred Haas also had his medical practice here before his licence was revoked in 1938. Source: Michael S. Phillips Archive.

Fig. 3.11 Bernhard Albert Mayer (b. 1866). Courtesy of Helen Mayer.

Fig. 3.12 49 Kaiserstrasse in 2012, former home of the Bernhard Mayer family. Bernhard Mayer specified these architectural details. The cartouche is a floor mosaic. Courtesy of Helen Mayer.

Fig. 3.13 2 Bauhofstrasse in 2012; the location of one of Bernhard Mayer's jewelry stores. Courtesy of Helen Mayer.

Fig. 3.14 Gestapo Headquarters. The corner house at 31 Kaiserstrasse was infamous during the Nazi era. Source: Michael S. Phillips Archive.

Fig. 3.15 Memorial at 31 Kaiserstrasse. Source: Michael S. Phillips Archive.

December 23, 1941

Mr. Lazaro Zelwer
Hias-Ica Emigration Assn.
Apartado Aereo 4261
Bogotá, Colombia

Dear Mr. Zelwer:

    We would like to confirm our yesterday's cable as
follows:

    "HUNDRED FORTYSEVEN WILL ARRIVE BARRANQUILLA END NEXT
    WEEK ACCOMPANIED BY GURFINKEL PLEASE PREPARE OVERNIGHT
    ACCOMODATIONS AVIANCA ARRANGING CONTINUATION TRIP ALSO
    OVERNIGHT ACCOMODATIONS CALI NEEDED FOR HUNDRED TWENTYTWO
    TWENTYFIVE OTHERS DESTINED COLOMBIA PLEASE NOTIFY RELA-
    TIVES OF ALL COLOMBIA LETTER FOLLOWS."

    Under great difficulties we have been able to arrange
to ship out 147 people destined to various South American
countries by making special arrangements with the Empresa
Naviera de Cuba to sail to Barranquilla. It was necessary
to make this arrangement rather than to follow any of your
suggestions because practically all of the people travelled
on German passports and the United Fruit Lines did not want
to take them through the Panama Canal. Furthermore, the other
lines which could have possibly been used did not have adequate
accomodations and it would have taken several months for our
people here to get out at the rate at which they were able to
take them. As far as the transportation from Barranquilla was
concerned, we had been informed by the Colombian Government
that they could issue transit visas valid for only 15 days
and that the Port of Buenaventura had been closed to all
ships so that in order to safe-guard the leaving of all those
in transit—within the prescribed period of time—it was necessary to make plane arrangements. The end result was the
arrangement with Avianca, under which Avianca has agreed to
put in special planes to take all the arrivals to Bogotá or
Ipiales respectively, a day after their arrival with a stop-
over in Cali.

Fig. 3.16 First two pages of a letter to HIAS-ICA Emigration Association in Bogotá about the arrival
of 147 German Jews, among them Siegbert and Estella Frohwein. Courtesy of the American Jewish
Joint Distribution Committee Archives.

- 2 -

Mr. Lazaro Zelwer   December 23, 1941

　　　Of the 147 persons, 27 are destined to Colombia, as
follows:

　　　　　　　　Olga DELLEVIE
　　　　　　　　Frieda WEILER
　　　　　　　　Anna SCHMOOG
　　　　　　　　Ellias & Elli SMOLINSKI
　　　　　　　　Lucie ZANDER
　　　　　　　　Jacob & Bertha KAHN
　　　　　　　　Ernst, Ida, Kurt and Ilse HEID
　　　　　　　　Walter, Emma & Daniel RAUSCH
　　　　　　　　Herman, Margarethe & Madeleine
　　　　　　　　　　　　　　GUGGENHEIM
　　　　　　　　Siegbert & Estela FROHWEIN
　　　　　　　　Olga DAVIDSON
　　　　　　　　Marie LIVSCHIN
　　　　　　　　Leopold & Selma KAHN
　　　　　　　　Veilchen APPEL
　　　　　　　　Rosel STRAUSS

　　　We would like you to know that the only accomodations
which we were able to get on the boat were half first class
and of the remainder, one-third each second and third class,
and the rest of the people we had to put on deck. However,
everybody in second and third and deck was to get the food of
the second class. Consequently, we made the space arrangements
in terms of: first, physically handicapped persons; second, the
very old people; third, families with small children; and fourth,
older couples. We did not take into consideration whose relatives did or did not pay all or part of the transportation,
because by the time the boat sailed we did not have complete
information in this respect.

　　　As a result, Jacob and Bertha Kahn were put first class
but the Heids and Mrs. Zander, third class. Also, you may
know that all except the Kahns and the Heids were held at the
Immigration Encampment Tiscornia from the day of their arrival
here until they left. In the case of Lucie Zander this was so
because while a Cuban Visa had been obtained for her, she left
Europe before the visa was actually stamped in her passport.

　　　In the following we would like to give you some further
information about some of the individuals who are destined to
Colombia.

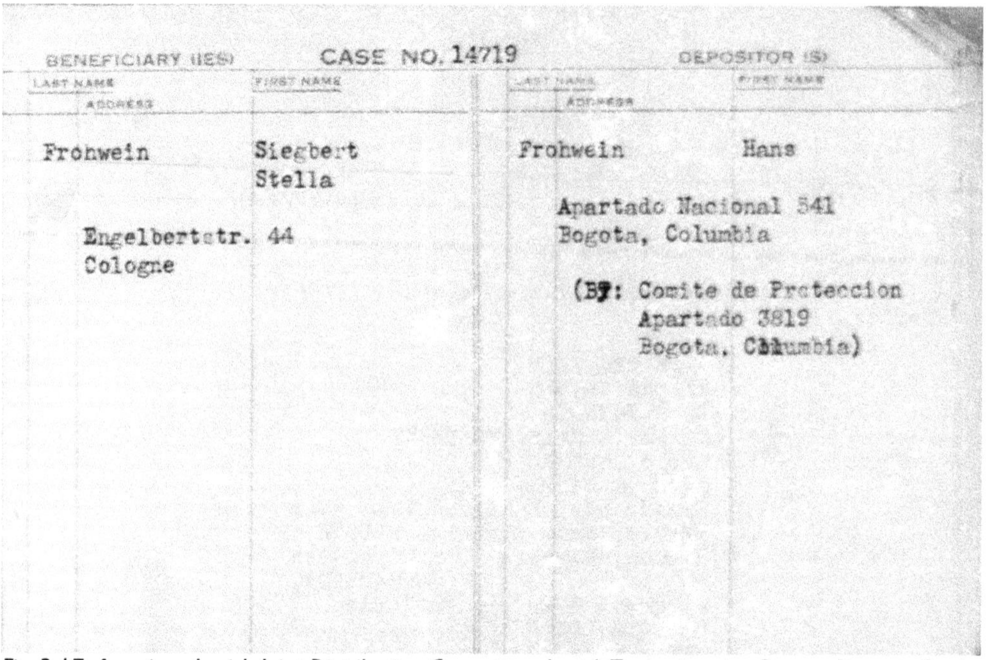

BENEFICIARY (IES)	CASE NO. 14719		DEPOSITOR (S)	
LAST NAME	FIRST NAME		LAST NAME	FIRST NAME
ADDRESS			ADDRESS	
Frohwein	Siegbert		Frohwein	Hans
	Stella			
			Apartado Nacional 541	
Engelbertstr. 44			Bogota, Columbia	
Cologne				
			(BY: Comite de Proteccion	
			Apartado 3819	
			Bogota, Columbia)	

Fig. 3.17 American Jewish Joint Distribution Committee, Jewish Transmigration Bureau Deposit Card for Siegbert Frohwein. The JDC's Transmigration Bureau helped Jews to emigrate from Europe by accepting funds from friends or family already abroad to pay for the travel costs of the individual seeking to leave. Source: American Joint Distribution Committee Archives and the Leo Baeck Institute.

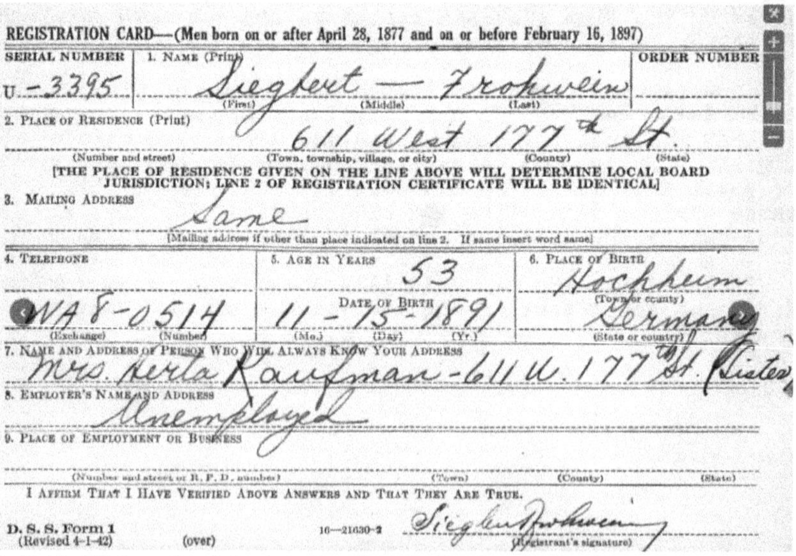

Fig. 3.18 US Army Draft Registration Card for Siegbert Frohwein.
Source: Ancestry.com.

Fig. 3.19 Early proof. Commemorative engraving of the Reform Synagogue by Hans Kohl, c.1920-1934. The synagogue was built in 1912, destroyed in Kristallnacht, 9-10 November 1938. The portraits are of Rabbi Sali Levi, installed 1919, and Bernhard Mayer, Congregation President. Courtesy of the Leo Baeck Institute.

Fig. 3.20 The synagogue's Moorish-style sanctuary, c.1918-1935. Courtesy of the Leo Baeck Institute.

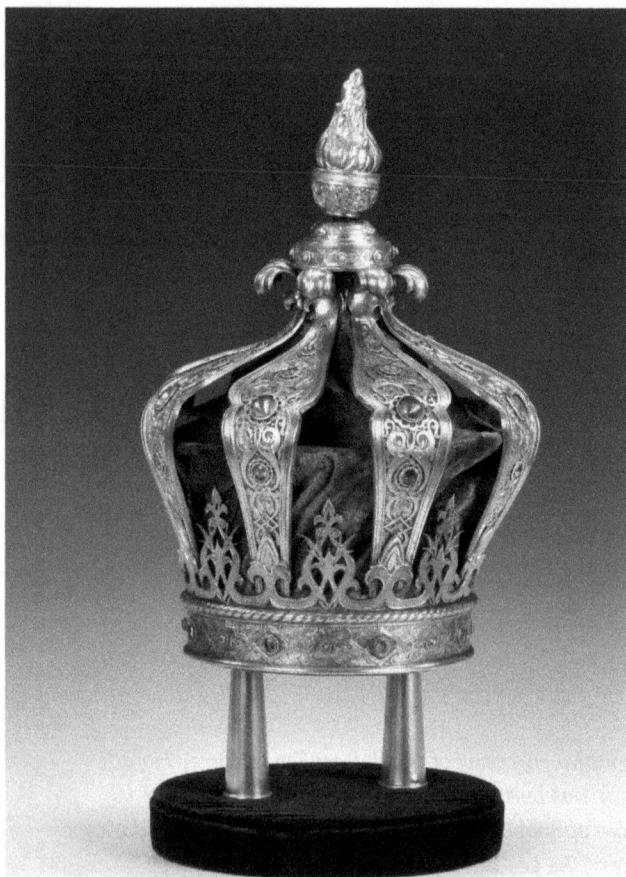

Fig. 3.21 Torah crown donated to the congregation by Martin Mayer's workshop in 1898. Source: GDKE RLP, Landesmuseum Mainz (U. Rudischer).

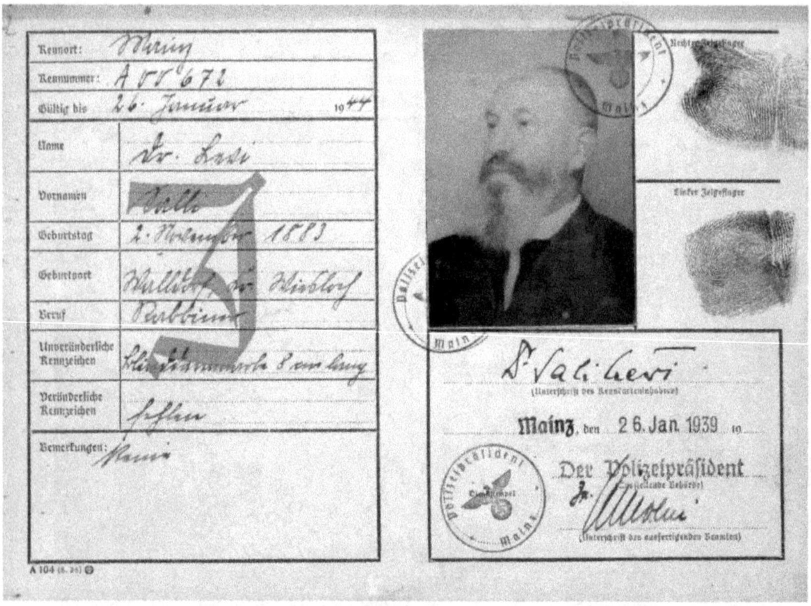

Kennort:

Kennummer:

Gültig bis

Name

Vornamen

Geburtstag

Geburtsort

Beruf

Unveränderliche Kennzeichen

Veränderliche Kennzeichen

Bemerkungen:

A 104

Linker Zeigefinger

(Unterschrift des Kennkarteninhabers)

Mainz, den 26. Jan. 1939

Der Polizeipräsident

(Unterschrift des ausfertigenden Beamten)

Fig. 3.22 Rabbi Dr. Sali Levi Kennkarte.
Source: Central Archive for the Study of the History of the Jews in Germany.

Chapter 4. Judenhäuser

After the war began, the situation for Jews remaining in Mainz grew even more perilous. Trapped, isolated and at risk, some managed to remain in their own homes, while others had been coerced into living in cramped shared accommodation with other Jews in a so-called judenhaus, or confined to the exclusively Jewish hospital, or one of the homes for elderly Jews.

My grandmother's uncle Paul Mayer (b. 1871) was in his late sixties when the war began. A former banker and shareholder in the Max Gutmann wine business, he was moved to a judenhaus at 13 Adam-Karrillon-Strasse, where he was, I believe, deprived of food and medical care, as well as his property and dignity. Since 1938, he had also been forced, like all Jewish men without readily identifiable Jewish names, to add the first name Israel on his identity card (women were forced to take the name Sara), and carry identity papers stamped with a large red J.[64]

Prior to Paul's death, he was moved to the Jewish Hospital at 11 Gonsenheimer Strasse where conditions were appalling. He died in 1941 of undocumented causes. Max and Rosalie Gutmann's eighth child Jenny Saarbach (b. 1863), who married into the family of Max's former business partner Eduard, had died in the same Jewish hospital the summer before. She was 77. Her sister Emma (b. 1858), who lived at 27 Kaiserstrasse, had already committed suicide in April 1939 by poisoning. I attribute the deaths of all these elderly people to the treatment they received under the Nazi regime that had made life intolerable for German Jews.

Anti-Jewish legislation became increasingly punitive. From September 1941, Jews were banned from public transport and any Jew aged six years and above was forced to wear a yellow star on their

outer clothing. Judenhäuser, like 13 Adam-Karrillon-Strasse, prolif-
erated. There was another on the same street at number 54, where
more than 40 people were barracked, and at 17 Walpodenstrasse, 25
Breidenbacherstrasse, 19, 21 and 28 Margaretengasse, 4 Frauenlob-
strasse and 45 Taunusstrasse.[65]

Number 32 Kaiserstrasse, where my grandmother spent her
childhood, was also to become a judenhaus with a compulsory black
Star of David displayed on the front door. The building stood in
convenient proximity to the Gestapo HQ at number 31 from where
the residents I am sure were kept under strict surveillance and control.

I am not certain what action my grandmother's mother Auguste
took from her house prior to her departure in early 1939, or how
it came to be a judenhaus. I only discovered that fact during my
research. But as of April 1938 all Jews had to report what property
they owned and also any assets worth more than 5,000 Reichmarks.
By the end of that year, the Decree on the Confiscation of Jewish
Property was issued to formalise the transfer of Jewish assets to
non-Jews.[66] She probably shared the fate of other Jewish homeown-
ers who remained living in houses stolen from them and forced to
pay rent. I suspect her departure in 1939 meant the building's new
non-Jewish or 'Aryan' landlords met no resistance as they took over
number 32. The building was already set up for multiple occupancy
having housed French officers on the upper floors after the First
World War.

I do know that the Bockmann and Loeb families were living at
32 Kaiserstrasse prior to their deportation in March 1942. Arthur
Bockmann (b. 1892), a wine merchant from Oppenheim, and his
wife Martha (b. 1888, née Mann) and his sisters Rosalie (b.1886) and
Johanna (b. 1883) and her son Robert Loeb (b. 1907) and his wife

Betty (b. 1906, née Epstein) and their son Werner Ludwig (b. 1931) were registered there. As Jews with connections to the wine trade, I believe the family was known to mine.

By 1942 Jews were also prohibited from entering certain areas in German cities, including particular shops and other public spaces, and had to contend with reduced rations once rationing began.[67] For Jews in Mainz, this was the year mass deportations started.[68] The Bockmanns and Loebs were—like Hildegard Heymann—on the first of the three major transports of Mainz Jews: the Da 14 train carrying 470 Mainz Jews bound for Trawniki in Poland, the nearest station to the Piaski ghetto, that left Darmstadt on 25 March 1942.

Johanna Loeb's husband Hugo Loeb (b. 1882) was spared the horrific fate of Piaski, having died of diabetes and calcification of his blood vessels in Mainz in February 1942. He is buried in the New Jewish Cemetery. Arthur and Martha Bockmann's only daughter Ruth (b. 1920) survived having fled to England in 1939 from where she travelled on to the US. In September 1940 she arrived in New York and made her way to Argentina. She died in Vermont in 1996.

Many of their Jewish neighbours from Kaiserstrasse were also herded onto the Da 14 train. These included Dr Walter Nathan (b. 1889), his wife Elisabeth (b. 1897, née August), Hans Daniel Nathan (b. 1936) and Lotte Emma Nathan (b. 1932), who were forced to reside at the judenhaus at number 21.

21 Kaiserstrasse was also the address where Rabbi Dr. Sali Levi (b. 1883) and his wife Margarete (b. 1886, née Weissmann), were housed before they fled to Berlin in 1941 hoping to obtain a visa for entry into the United States. Levi, undoubtedly under significant strain, suffered a heart attack before he could depart and died in April 1941. Margarete made it to the US where she died in 1960.

Adolf Kahn (b. 1864) had resided there before he was transferred to the Jewish Hospital, where he died in May 1941, perhaps assisted by the staff.

Number 32 and 21 served as holding pens as the deportations gathered speed. Emil Julius Seligmann (b. 1866) from Oppenheim and his wife Margarete (b. 1874, née Heil), known as Grete, were housed at 32 Kaiserstrasse until they were deported to Theresienstadt, where Emil died in December 1942 and his wife the following May. They were on the second of the mass transportations from Mainz. The train left Darmstadt on 27 September 1942 destined for Terezin station, close to Theresienstadt.[69] About 1,300 people from Hesse were crammed aboard, among them 453 from Mainz.[70]

The mass deportation to Theresienstadt was followed by the third major transport of Mainz Jews eastward that occurred just days later. This time, on 30 September, almost 900 people from Hessia were (probably) taken to the Treblinka extermination camp north east of Warsaw, in Poland.[71] Irma Kahn (b. 1998, née Kahn) and her husband Dr. Fritz Kahn (b. 1901), who had lived at number 21 Kaiserstrasse, were deported from 54 Adam-Karrillon-Strasse, one of the judenhäuser, with their son Erich (b. 1929). They are likely to have been murdered at Treblinka soon after their arrival.

Transit

Unknown to me prior to having started researching the Jewish residents of Kaiserstrasse before and during the War, the acclaimed German novelist, writer and activist Anna Seghers (b. 1900 as Netty Reiling), and her parents Isidor (b.1867) and Hedwig Reiling (b. 1880, née Fuld) lived at 34 Kaiserstrasse, next door to my grandmother's childhood home.[72] Milly and Netty were only six years apart in age and Netty was the same age as my grandmother's sister Anna. I do not know if the Gutmanns and Reilings knew each other but it would seem odd, given the intertwined nature of the Jewish households on that street, if they did not.

Isidor and his elder brother Hermann Reiling (b. 1862) were partners in an art and antique dealing business.[73] Netty was brought up in an Orthodox household. She studied at the University of Heidelberg from 1920 until 1924, where she obtained a doctorate in art history, met Ladislaus Rádványi (1900–1978), a Hungarian Jew, communist and her future husband, and began writing fiction.[74] By the time she joined the German Communist Party in 1928, she had two children. The family left Germany a few years later, heading first for Zürich and then Paris in 1933.[75] Upon the Nazi occupation of northern France, the family emigrated again, this time eventually landing in Mexico having been denied entry into the US. From there she organised a visa for her mother but it was too late.[76]

Isidor and Hedwig (known as Heddy) had moved from 34 Kaiserstrasse around 1933 and were living at 23 Fischtorplatz in Mainz. Prior to deportation on the 25 March 1942 train to Piaski, Hedwig was registered at 31 Taunusstrasse. She did not survive. By this time, Isidor was dead, having passed away in the Jewish Hospital in March 1940. His brother Hermann and his wife Flora (b. 1869, née Rosenthal) were confined to a room at 53 Kaiserstrasse at some point I believe after 1939 and were moved again, this time to 32 Kaiserstrasse. Hermann died on 30 March 1942 in Mainz. Flora was deported to Theresienstadt on 27 September that year. She died there in February 1943.

Much of Seghers' work addresses the rise of fascism and the grip of National Socialism on German politics and society between the wars. Of her novels, *The Seventh Cross*, published in 1942 (and made into a Hollywood film), is mainly set in (fictitious) Westhofen, one of the early concentration camps, and describes the attempt of seven prisoners to escape from the camp. *The Excursion of the Dead Girls* (written in Mexico in 1943-44 and published in 1946) recounts a school outing on the Rhine after the First World War and the differing fates of the children in the years to come. In her novel *Transit*, her protagonist has escaped a concentration camp and is a refugee waiting in Marseilles (France) for a boat to leave Europe. Seghers returned to Germany in 1947 and settled in East Berlin in 1950. She died in June 1983.[77]

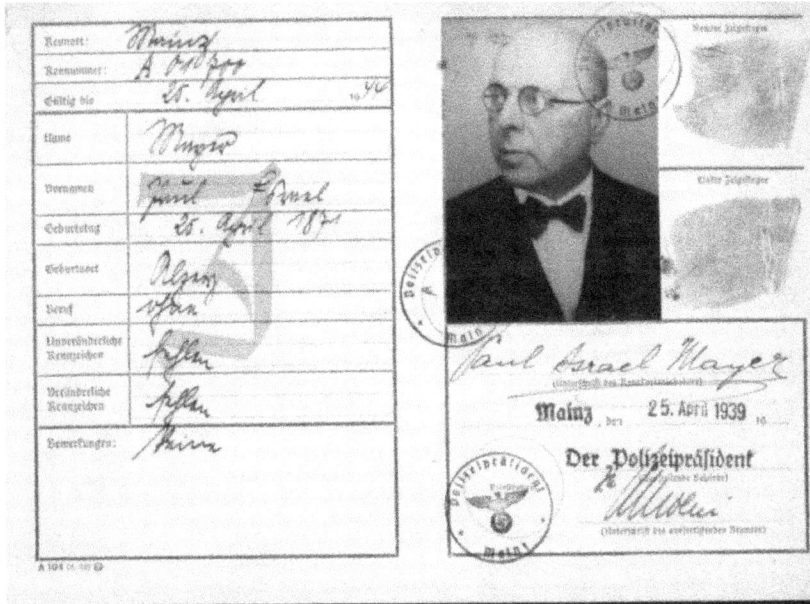

Fig. 4.1 Paul Mayer Kennkarte.
After the war began, my grandmother's uncle was forcibly housed at 54 Adam-Karrillon-Strasse, just around the corner from Kaiserstrasse. Source: Central Archive for the Study of the History of the Jews in Germany.

Fig. 4.2 13 Adam-Karrillon-Strasse. It had belonged to the wine merchant Siegmund Vogel. The building next to it was also taken over and used as a judenhaus. Photo by Schwalbner, via Wikipedia.org.

Fig. 4.3 Robert Loeb Kennkarte.
Source: Central Archive for the Study of the History of the Jews in Germany.

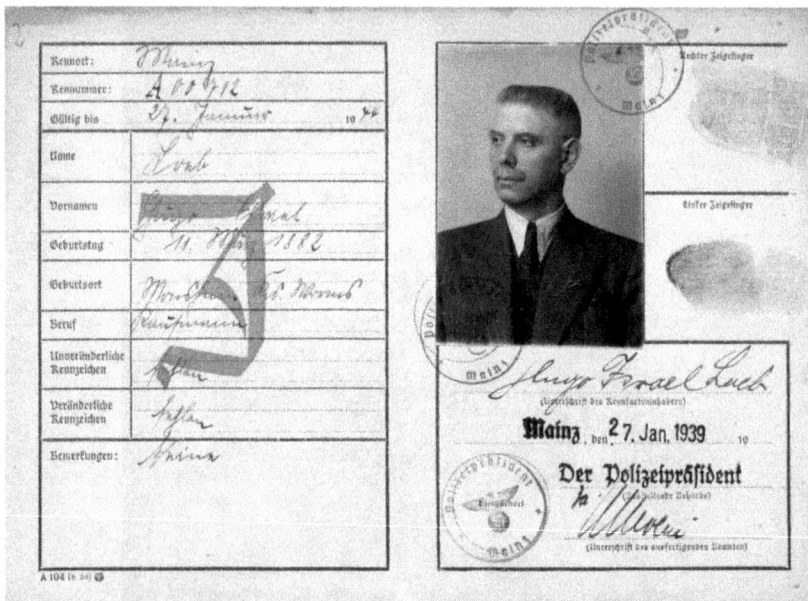

Fig. 4.4 Hugo Loeb Kennkarte.
Source: Central Archive for the Study of the History of the Jews in Germany.

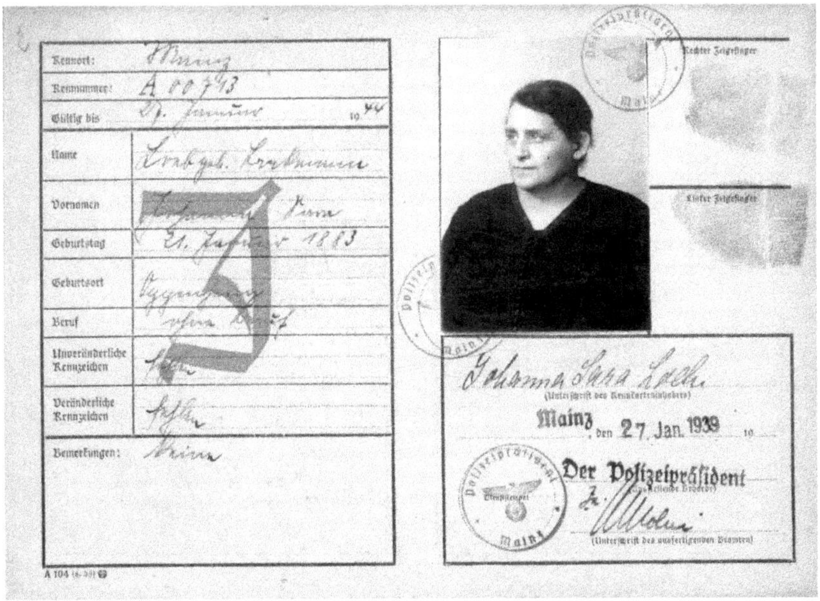

Fig. 4.5 Johanna Loeb Kennkarte.
Jewish women without readily identifiable Jewish names were obliged to adopt the
middle name Sara. Source: Central Archive for the Study of the History of the Jews
in Germany.

Fig. 4.6 Ruth Regina Bockmann, from her
kennkarte. Leaving her parents behind,
Ruth arrived in Argentina in 1940 aged
20 before settling in the US where she
lived with her husband Carl Freitag and
their child. Courtesy of Dennis Aron.

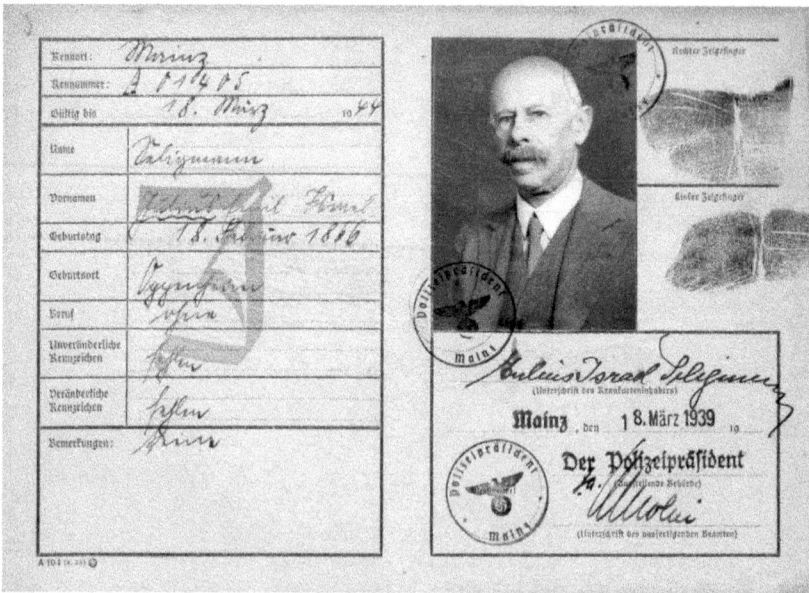

Fig. 4.7 Emil Julius Seligmann Kennkarte.
Source: Central Archive for the Study of the History of the Jews in Germany.

Fig. 4.8 Nathan Family Stolpersteine, 24 Kaiserstrasse. Photo by Nixnubix
via Wikipedia.org.

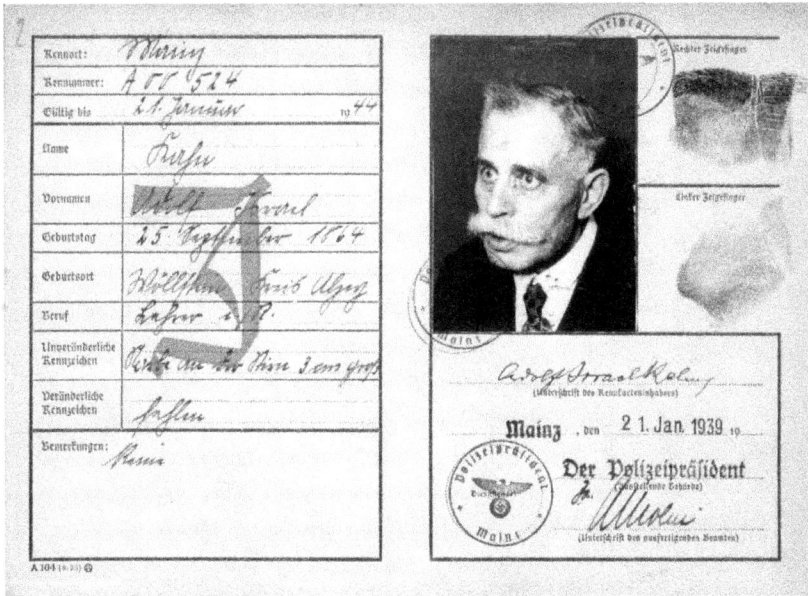

Fig. 4.9 Adolf Kahn Kennkarte.
Source: Central Archive for the Study of the History of the Jews in Germany.

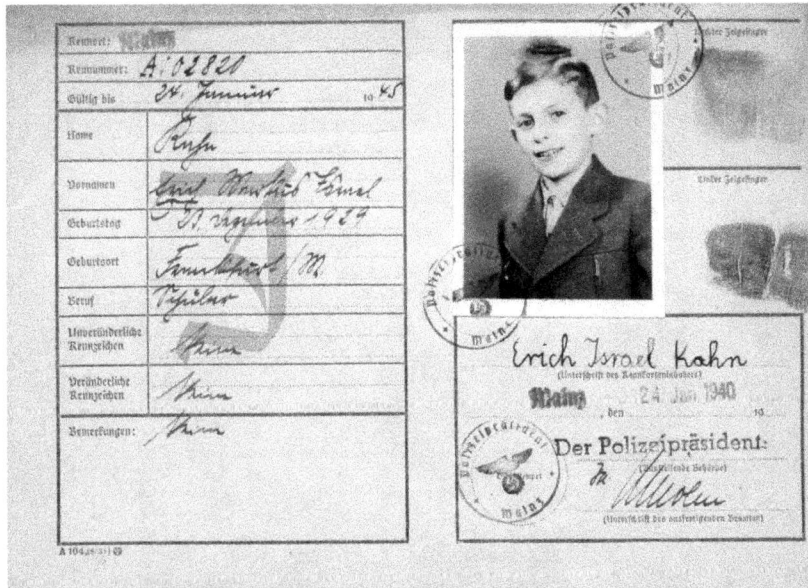

Fig. 4.10 Erich Kahn Kennkarte
Source: Central Archive for the Study of the History of the Jews in Germany.

Fig. 4.11 Netty and Hedwig Reiling. Source: Mainz City
Archives, Reference: BPSF/595 D.

Fig. 4.12 Anna Seghers in 1975. Photo by Horst Sturm
via Wikipedia.org.

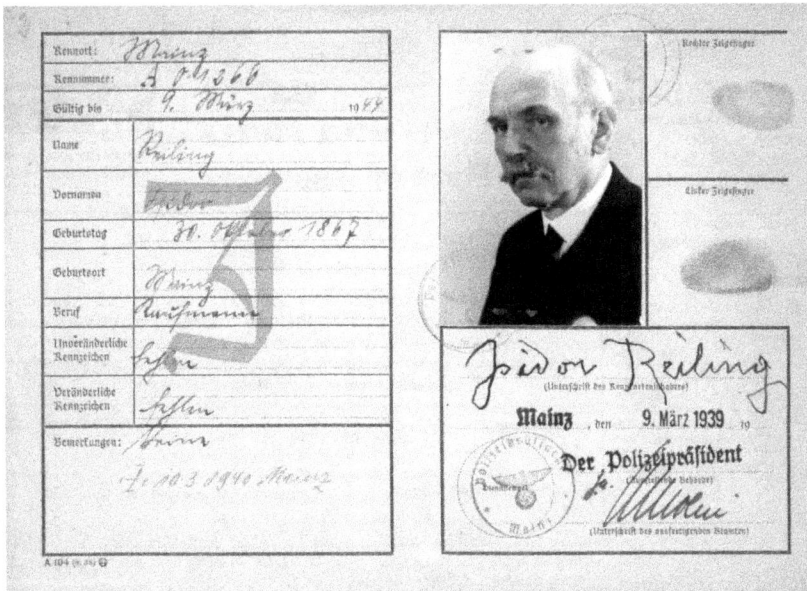

Fig. 4.13 Isidor Reiling Kennkarte.
Source: Central Archive for the Study of the History of the Jews in Germany.

Fig. 4.14 Grave of Rabbi Dr Sali Levi, Jewish Cemetery,
Weissensee-Berlin. Levi died in Berlin in 1941 en route to the US.
Source: Ancestry.com.

YAD VASHEM
Martyrs' and Heroes'
Remembrance
Authority
P.O.B. 84 Jerusalem, Israel

דף־עד
עדות־בלאט
A Page of Testimony

THE MARTYRS' AND
HEROES' REMEMBRANCE
LAW, 5713—1953
determines in article No. 2
that —
The task of YAD VASHEM
is to gather into the homeland
material regarding all those
members of the Jewish people
who laid down their lives, who
fought and rebelled against the
Nazi enemy and his collaborators, and to perpetuate their
memory and that of the
communities, organisations, and
institutions which were destroyed because they were Jewish.

1. Family name * **Reiling**

2. First Name (maiden name) **Fuld Heddy** (mother of the author Anna Seghers)

3. Date of birth | 4. Place of birth (town, country) **Frankfurt a/M Germany**

5. Name of father **Sally Fuld** | 6. Name of mother **Hedde Fuld**

7. Name of spouse (if a wife, add maiden name) **Lutz Reiling - Fuld**

8. Place of residence before the war **Mainz Germany**

9. Places of residence during the war ✓

10. Circumstances of death (place, date, etc.) **Concentration camp**

I, the undersigned **Regina Blanche Rosenberger**

residing at (full address) **1040 Sheppard Ave E #1906**

relationship to deceased **Cousin**

hereby declare that this testimony is correct to the best of my knowledge.

Place and date **Willowdale Ont. Sept. 18th**   Signature **Regina R. Rosenberg**

"...ונתתי להם בביתי ובחומתי יד ושם...אשר לא יכרת:" (ישעיה נו, ה)
**"...even unto them will I give in mine house and within my
walls a place and a name...that shall not be cut off."** (Isaiah, LVI,5)

* Please inscribe the name of each victim of the Holocaust on a separate form.

Fig. 4.15 Page of Testimony for Hedwig 'Heddy' Reiling.
Heddy's cousin Regina Rosenberger filed this Page of Testimony. Before Hedwig was deported to
Piaski, she was registered at 32 Kaiserstrasse. Source: Yad Vashem Hall of Names.

Chapter 5. The Murdered

In many cases it is not obvious when individuals took up residence on Kaiserstrasse, or their relationship or connection to the other families with whom they shared accommodation. Many of the properties were large, and if they were like my grandmother's childhood home at number 32, had been divided into units following the First World War ready for multiple-occupancy. Undoubtedly this was a benefit the Nazis recognised and of which they took advantage.

The movements of Franziska Nachmann (b. 1918, née Mayer), who appeared on the 1939 census at number 53, are an example of how fluid the situation was for Jews at the time, and how individuals moved around as they sought safety or were forcibly taken to different addresses.

As far as I can determine, she is not directly linked to the family of prominent community leader Bernhard Albert Mayer (b. 1866), who was associated with the house through the Martin Mayer jewellery business and left for Buenos Aires in March 1941 with his wife Adele (b. 1873). I suspected she was put there simply because she shared a surname.

Franziska was the daughter of Julius Mayer (b. 1882) and Clementine (b. 1885, née Bodenheimer). According to Horst Kasper, a researcher based in Bodenheim near Mainz, her place of birth, Franziska was brought up in modest circumstances and worked as a waitress in a café in Mainz. While the 1939 census puts her at 53 Kaiserstrasse, before her marriage she lived at 32 Flachsmarkt. By 1941 she was married and living at 15 Leibnizstrasse with her husband Joseph Nachmann, according to Kasper.

Both husband and wife were in possession of exit documents and had travel tickets when Franziska was arrested, Kasper discovered.

Franziska and her husband were sent to Piaski in 1942 on the 25 March transport. Joseph (who was never registered at number 53) died in 1942 at the Majdanek concentration camp on the outskirts of the city of Lublin in Poland not far from Piaski. Franziska died at Piaski.

Franziska's father Julius Mayer died in Auschwitz in May 1944, while her mother Clementine survived the war and died in Alsace in 1948. Their son Lothar (b. 1913), Franziska's brother, had emigrated to Palestine in 1935.

Another Mayer living at number 53 was Albert Mayer (b. 1874), Bernhard Albert Mayer's cousin, who, with his brother Ernst Mayer (b. 1878), assisted Bernhard Albert with the family jewellery business. Albert fled to France in 1939 where he was later arrested. He was killed at Auschwitz in December 1943.

Albert's wife Emma Mayer (b. 1887, née Lauinger) had also arrived in France in 1939, travelled on to Switzerland and had made it to the US by 1940. She could have been in the company of their daughters Jula Mayer (b. 1910) and Margot Weinbach (b. 1913, née Mayer) who took the same route around the same time.

Both daughters lived long lives. Jula died in New York in 1983, while Margot, known as Margrit, who fled first to France in 1939, appears to have returned there. She died there in 2004. She was awarded France's Medal of Resistance on 23 Oct 1945. Albert and Emma's son Bernhard Albert Mayer (b. 1914) left Mainz in 1937. He appears to have joined his family in the US and died in New York in 1986.

Another resident of number 53, Helene Heinemann (b. 1878)—like Franziska, I do not know her connection to the Mayer family—left for Sweden in 1939.

Karl Schloss (b. 1876) was also recorded as living at number 53 before he fled to the Netherlands. Following his arrest, he was murdered at Auschwitz in January 1944. However, Karl's wife Lina Schloss (b. 1875, née Liebenstein) survived, arriving in the US at some point before 1949 before moving on to Rio de Janeiro in 1951. By then she was an elderly widow compelled to start a new life in a foreign place.

Also living at number 53 for a short period were Frieda Jourdan (b. 1886) and her sister Johanna Jourdan (b. 1891) after this property had become a judenhaus. They were last registered at 32 Kaiserstrasse before they were deported to Treblinka on the transport that left on 30 September 1942.

Those with Frieda and Johanna on this final mass transport from Mainz must have been under no illusion about their fate. They had already been or seen their neighbours being shunted from property to property and then disappear and never return. They may have even received correspondence from relatives who had been sent to Piaski and Theresienstadt earlier and were desperate for help.[78]

The family of Salomon (Sally) Haas (b. 1879) at number 74 Kaiserstrasse exemplify this pattern of moving people from house to house and separating families prior to deportation. Sally lived with his sister Klara Koch (b. 1877, née Haas), his daughter Alice Klara Maria Haas (b. 1908), his son Emil Jakob Haas (b. 1905) and Emil's wife Martha (b. 1898, née Strauss). Sally's wife Maria had died in 1935. Klara's husband Albert Koch (b. 1877) had been taken from the house in late 1940 and died that December.

After then, the family was probably all moved to the judenhaus at 58 Adam-Karrillon-Strasse. By the summer of 1941, Klara and Alice shared a room there. In March 1942, Emil, Martha and Alice were deported to Piaski. Emil may have died at Majdanek. Before

Sally Haas and Klara Koch were deported to Theresienstadt on the 27 September transport, they were moved to a judenhaus at 91/10 Schiessgartenstrasse. Sally died at Theresienstadt in May 1943 aged 64. Klara died there the following April.

Friedrich Karl Buschhoff (b. 1891) from Worms was also registered at 74 Kaiserstrasse. He was sent to Buchenwald in September 1943. He died in January 1945 at a labour camp.

Age No Bar

Many of the Kaiserstrasse residents loaded on to the goods trains destined ultimately for the concentration or extermination camps were very elderly. It is possible they were too old or infirm to flee, or equally likely they could not obtain exit permits or entry visas to safe countries in time.

Moritz Oppenheim (b. 1877) and his wife Marie Oppenheim (b. 1881, née Landauer) lived at number 82 before they were moved to 16 Eleonorenstrasse at Mainz-Kastel and then deported on the first mass transport, the Da 14 train that left Darmstadt on 25 March and would take them to Piaski. Moritz was approaching his 65th birthday. Marie was 60.

Heinrich Wolff (b.1878) and his wife Selma (b. 1883, née Hecht) of 29 Kaiserstrasse were on the same train, which left on his 64th birthday. Selma was 59 years old. They did not survive. They had fled from Nackenheim, a wine-growing village near Mainz, in the 1930s, seeking safety in the city. Regina Schmidt (b. 1879, née Wendel) who lived at the same address was on the same transport.

Gustav Blum (b. 1865) was 77 years old and his wife Charlotte Blum (b. 1875, née Mainzer) was 67 when they died at Theresienstadt in January and March 1943 respectively. They had lived in an apartment at number 24 Kaiserstrasse, with Simon Gaertner (b. 1861) and his wife Juliane Gaertner (b. 1859, née Blum), who was a relative, before they were moved to 17 Walpodenstrasse, another judenhaus. Simon died in July 1940 in Mainz. Juliane was 83 when she died at Theresienstadt. Robert Blum (b. 1880)—who was also likely a relation, although I have not be able to prove this—died in the Lodz ghetto in August 1942 aged 62.

Joel Emrich (b. 1867), who lived at 27 Kaiserstrasse with his wife Pauline (b. 1877, née Mann), died in Theresienstadt in March 1943, aged 76. Pauline managed to escape and passed away in the US years later in 1964. Ludwig Friedmann (b. 1882) and his sister Anna Jackobine Friedmann also lived at number 27. Ludwig had fled to France where he was arrested and deported to Auschwitz in August 1942. Ludwig's son Martin (b. 1924) had already fled to Switzerland in April 1939.

Up the street at number 55, Karoline Metzger (b. 1874, née Jung) was aged 68 when she was deported to Theresienstadt at the end of September 1942. She was last registered at 31 Taunusstrasse.

Albert Fried (b. 1870), who lived at number 66, with his wife, Frieda (b. 1877, née Schnurmann) died at Theresienstadt in January and July 1943, respectively. Albert was in his early seventies and Frieda not much younger. Their children Theo (b. 1902) and Emma (b. 1905) survived. Theo arrived in Bolivia in June 1939, while Emma arrived in the UK in the same month.

Georg August Mayer (b. 1878) lived at 94 Kaiserstrasse, the same building as Carl Theodor Frank who was betrayed by his tenant. Georg died in October 1942 aged 64 at Theresienstadt; a matter of days after the September transport arrived.

Arthur Nathan Kahn (b. 1867), also formerly of 94 Kaiserstrasse was 75 when in September 1942 he was taken from 25 Breidenbach-erstrasse, the Jewish home for the elderly. He died at Theresienstadt in October 1942. His wife Bertha Kahn (b. 1875, née Blum) died there in January 1944. Karl Herz (b. 1869) and his wife Adele Herz (b. 1880, née Mayer) lived at the same address. Adele died at Theresienstadt also in January 1944, followed by Karl in June. Karl would have been in his mid-seventies. Their much younger neighbour or possible maid Ingeborg (Inge) Henlein (b. 1921) had already been taken on the March 1942 transport to Piaski. She had just celebrated her 21st birthday.

Karl and Adele's sons Franz Max Herz (b. 1902) and Alfred Emil Herz (b. 1906) had fled to England in August and September of 1939. Alfred continued on to the US. Anna Ketch (b. 1870, née Herz) lived at the same address and was probably a relative. In 1944, she also arrived in the US.

Separated Endings

By now it should be clear that not all residents of the same address or members of the same family suffered the same end. Isaac Jo-seph Fulda (b. 1868) and his wife Johanna (b. 1874, née Rosenblatt), their son Ernst (b. 1899) and granddaughter Margot (b. 1930) fled 38 Kaiserstrasse in August 1939 for the Netherlands. Margot's father Leonhard Fulda had died in 1937. However, the war was to catch up with them. Ernst was taken to Auschwitz in September 1942, where he died. Isaak, Johanna and Margot were shipped to Sobibor in May 1943 where they were murdered. Their neighbour Martin Koch (b. 1872) of number 35 had also fled to the Netherlands in 1940. He was murdered in Auschwitz in November 1942.

Isaak Jacob Schamroth-Landau (b. 1895) who lived at number 80 Kaiserstrasse was born in Krakow. He too was to end his days at Auschwitz, where he died in March 1942. However, records show that his wife Regina 'Rivka' Schamroth-Landau (b. 1897, née Fendler), also born in Krakow, died in December 1943 at Tarnow, a city east of Krakow that before the war was home to a sizeable Jewish population. As the war progressed, the city was the scene of mass murder, deportations, selections and the establishment of a Jewish ghetto.[79] The ghetto was destroyed in September 1943 and remaining residents were sent to Auschwitz or Plaszow extermination camps.[80]

Isaak and Rivka's daughters, Frieda 'Frida' Schamroth-Landau (b. 1924) and Edith 'Ester' Schamroth-Landau (b. 1927), both born in Germany, died at some point between 1942 and 1945 in Krakow.

At the beginning of the War, 80 Kaiserstrasse was also home to Rieka Lämmel (b. 1893, née Kirchheimer) and her children Hella Lämmel (b. 1916) and Gerd Lämmel (b. 1920), who all died in Auschwitz in 1943. Rieka's husband Max Lämmel (b. 1884) was a Protestant who had died in 1928, according to investigations conducted by Mainz-based researcher Reinhard Frenzel. As Hella and Gerd were brought up as Jewish, under Nazi race laws they were denied the protection of a 'privileged mixed marriage' in Nazi jargon, even though their mother had married a non-Jew.[81] In December 1942 Hella was cautioned by the Gestapo for allegedly hiding the yellow star all Jews were compelled to wear on their outer garments. At some point the family was moved to an apartment at 3 Gartenfeldstrasse. According to Frenzel's research, Hella was arrested in April 1943, when the family was living at 21 Margaretengasse, and sent to Auschwitz. (As were her mother and brother.)

Died in Mainz

Some Kaiserstrasse residents, primarily the very old and the sick, passed away or committed suicide before the transports could take them to their deaths. I do not consider their endings benign. Deprived of food, healthcare, dignity and liberty, they either gave up or decided to take matters into their own hands.

Emma Frederike Neumann (b. 1858, née Gutmann) was one of Max Gutmann's six daughters. My great grandmother Auguste was married to Max's cousin Ferdinand, and lived close by. I believe she would have known Emma well. The older lady lived at number 27 Kaiserstrasse with her husband Bernhard Neumann (b. 1847). Around the same time my grandmother Milly was leaving for England, in April 1939, Emma committed suicide by ingesting Veronal (a barbiturate) and coal gas. Bernhard died the following January, perhaps of starvation.

The Salomons lived at 37 Kaiserstrasse. Before the family shoe business was forcibly sold to a non-Jewish employee, it had supported a very wealthy lifestyle for Fritz Siegfried Salomon (b. 1879), his wife Anny Bertha Salomon (b. 1888, née Baer) and their daughter Gertrude (b. 1918). Like the Gutmanns, they had a cook and a nanny and Gertrude attended the same high school as my grandmother, albeit at a later date.[82]

As a young woman, Gertrude worked at a Jewish restaurant and a Jewish school, while she planned their escape to Switzerland. She was arrested in 1939, during which time (in July 1939) her father killed himself.[83] After her release, she obtained the transit visa required to travel to Shanghai from where she sought a visa for Cuba for her mother. It arrived too late. Anny was deported to Piaski in March 1942 and murdered at Treblinka. Gertrude remained in China for the duration of the war.

Alice Kronenberger (b. 1878, née Kaufmann), who lived at 55 Kaiserstrasse, died in 1941 in Mainz of suspected suicide. She is buried in the New Jewish Cemetery with her first husband Theodor Levi Morreau (b. 1871) who died in 1916. During her first marriage, she shared the same name as my grandmother's great friend and sponsor Alice Morreau (née Weinmann) who provided for and supported her and her children when they arrived in England in 1939 and for years after. Following Theodor's death, Alice married Hermann Kronenberger, a member of the German banking dynasty that owned an impressive establishment at 35-37 Grosse Bleiche.

Eugenie Rosalie Jourdan (b. 1873, née Gudenburg) lived at 66 Kaiserstrasse. She died in May 1939, four years after her husband Siegfried and just before the war began. It appears she starved to death.

The deaths on the same day, 27 September 1944, of three residents of 82 Kaiserstrasse: Else Besier (b. 1897, née Asnes) and her daughter Hildegard Besier, who was classified as half Jewish (b. 1930) and Klementine Eugenie Sauer (b. 1885, née Fridburg), were due to 'enemy action', meaning they died in an Allied air raid. Hildegard's older sister Irmgard Besier survived the war.

At number 36, Emma Neumann's sister Ida Wilhelmine Bing (b. 1867, née Gutmann)—who would also have been known to Auguste and Milly—starved to death in May 1941. Her husband, Judge Simon Otto Bing (b. 1863) had died in 1937. Their daughter Elisabeth Mayer (b. 1894), a doctor, and her husband Ernst Joseph Mayer (b. 1885) died in Theresienstadt in 1943.

A number of esteemed individuals who had devoted their lives to public service lived on the street. Dr Moritz Karl Goldschmidt (b. 1873) lived at number 50 Kaiserstrasse. The former district court director was unmarried and had no children, according to research conducted by Tillmann Krach.[84] On the questionnaire he was obliged to complete upon the introduction of the Law for the Restoration of the Professional Civil Service in April 1933, which would ultimately ban all those classified as Jewish from holding official positions, Goldschmidt noted that his parents Eduard and Rosalie Goldschmidt were baptised Protestants.[85] This apparently carried little weight with the Nazis and he was forced to retire in 1933 if he was to retain his pension for 39 years of service.[86]

Prior to his death, he was compulsorily moved from number 50 Kaiserstrasse to the judenhaus at number 21 before he was admitted to the Jewish Hospital at Gonsenheimer Strasse. His death certificate details 'sleeping pill poisoning' and suggests that he committed suicide.[87] He died on 30 March 1942, five days after the first mass deportation headed for the Piaski ghetto.

Eduard Strauss (b. 1869) was 70 when the war began. He was also sent from pillar to post, moving from 80 Kaiserstrasse to 3 Gartenfeldstrasse in 1940 to another judenhaus on Adam-Karrillon-Strasse and then on to the Jewish Hospital at Gonsenheimer Strasse, where he died in February 1942. His death certificate cites artherosclerosis (narrowing of the arteries) as the cause. Such a terrorised and unsettled life could not have helped the old man's health.

Jacob (b. 1972) and Rosa Deutsch (b. 1880, née Lorch) lived at 19 Kaiserstrasse. Jacob died in May 1940, I speculate of a combination of stress and starvation, and is buried in Mainz's New Jewish Cemetery. Rosa managed to evade the Nazis and appears to have passed away in Vienna in 1947 on her way to Argentina.

However, the end of the war did not bring the end of suffering. Milly Franziska Mathilde Schiffner (b. 1902, née Lekisch) of number

42 must have been one of the last Jews left in Mainz when the war ended in September 1945. She did not live long enough to see the city restored. She died in April 1949 aged 47 of suspected starvation.

During their long lifetimes, the elderly residents of Kaiserstrasse witnessed great changes in the status of the Jewish community in Mainz. When they were children, many were for the better, but undoubtedly, in their latter years, all of them for the very much worse. Adolf Kern (b. 1937), who died in Mainz in March 1940, registered at 82 Kaiserstrasse, was two years old when he passed away. He would only have known starvation and deprivation.

Fig. 5.1 The Holocaust in Occupied Poland
Source: Wikimedia Commons/Dennis Nilsson. Public domain.

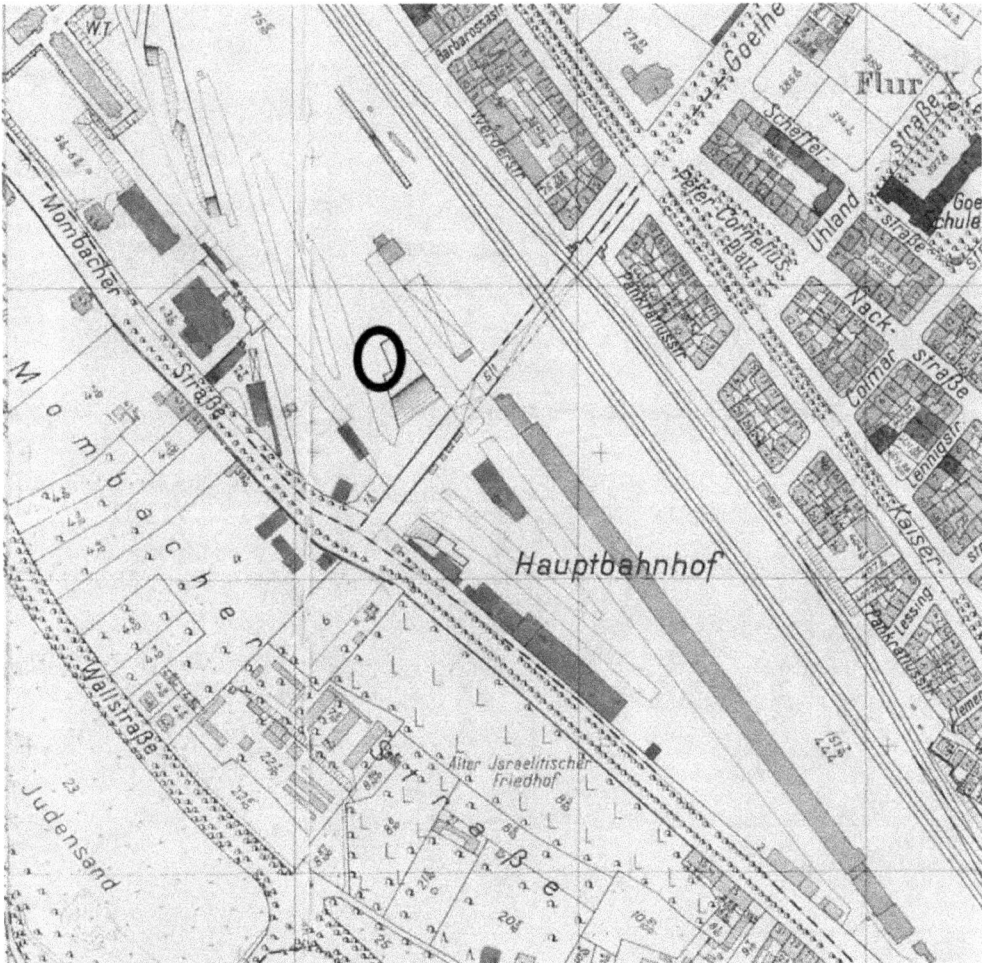

Fig. 5.2 Position of the Deportation Ramp at the Main Train Station in Mainz.
The Old Jewish Cemetery is located directly opposite. Source: Mainz City Archives,
Reference: BPSP/595 D.

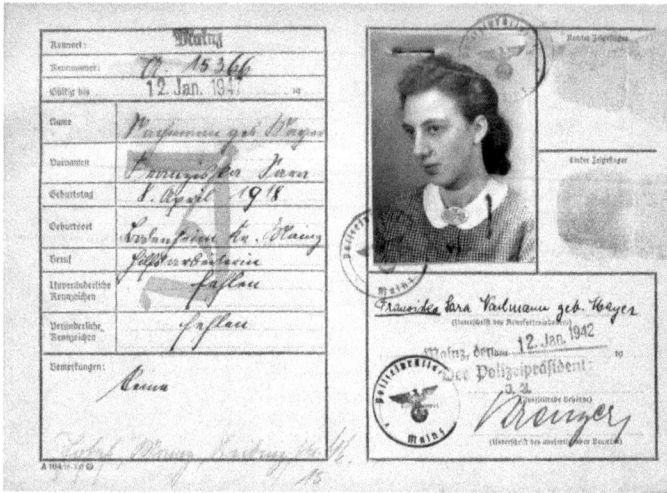

Fig. 5.3 Franziska Nachmann (née Mayer) Kennkarte. Source: Central Archive for the Study of the History of the Jews in Germany.

Fig. 5.4 Joseph Nachmann Kennkarte. Franziska's husband who died at Majdanek Concentration Camp in Poland. Source: Central Archive for the Study of the History of the Jews in Germany.

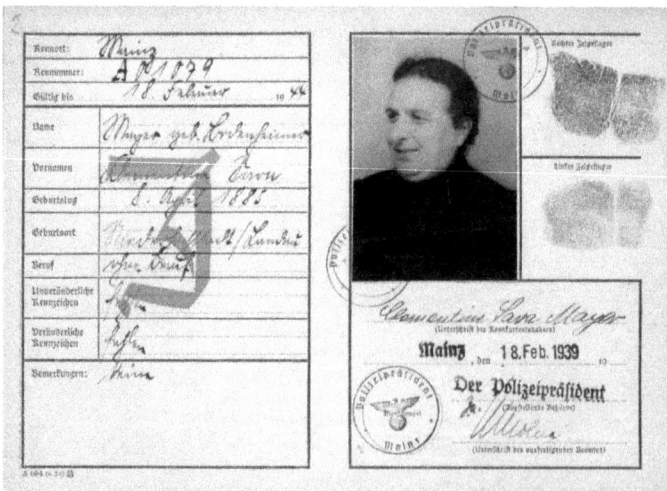

Fig. 5.5 Clementine Mayer Kennkarte. Mother of Franziska Nachmann. Source: Central Archive for the Study of the History of the Jews in Germany.

Fig. 5.6 Postcard from Piaski. Moritz Fried writes from the Piaski ghetto-transit camp near Lublin in April 1942 a month after the first mass deportation of Jews from Mainz. The card is addressed to Michel Oppenheim, 21 Kaiserstrasse. Source: Mainz City Archives, Reference: NL Oppenheim /49,5, site 8.

Fig. 5.7 Stolpersteine for the Mayer Family, 53 Kaiserstrasse. Photos by Nixnubix via Wikipedia.org.

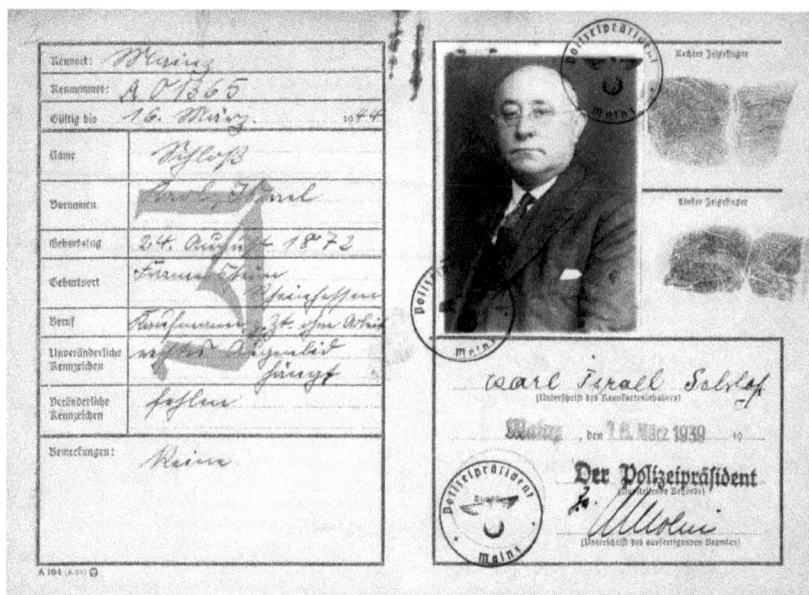

Fig. 5.8 Karl Schloss Kennkarte.
Source: Central Archive for the Study of the History of the Jews in Germany.

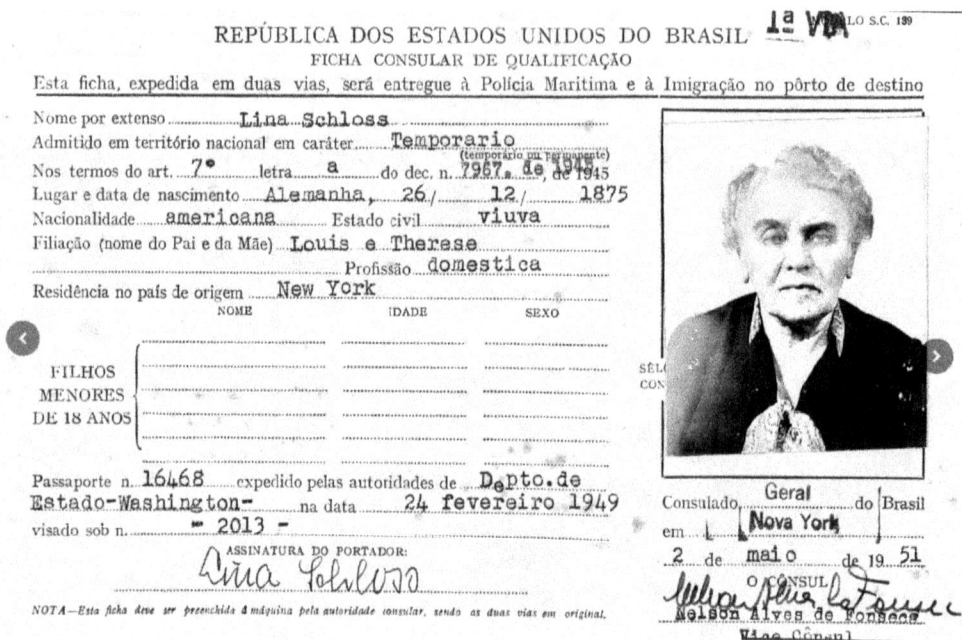

Fig. 5.9 Brazilian Entry Visa. Lina Schloss, Karl's wife, arrived in Rio de Janeiro from New York in 1951 aged 75. Source: Ancestry.com.

Fig. 5.10 Salomon (Sally) Haas Kennkarte.
Source: Central Archive for the Study of the History of the Jews in Germany.

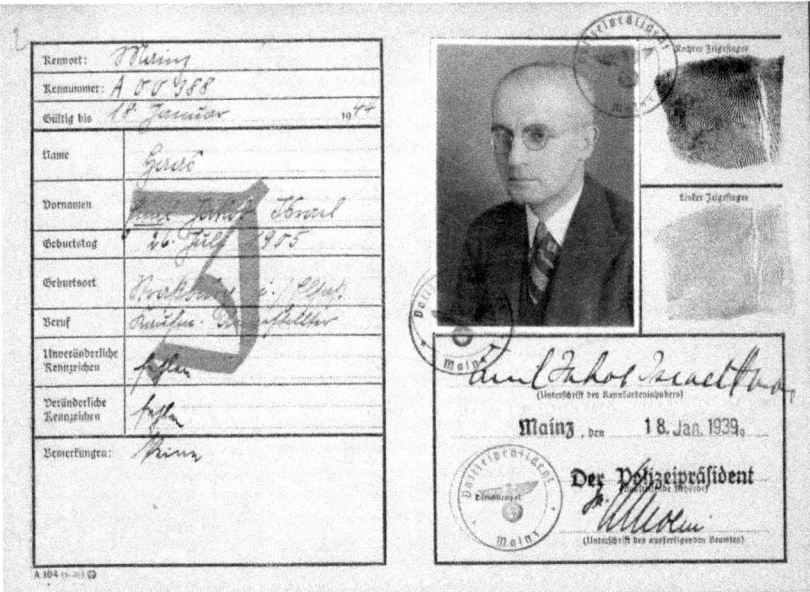

Fig. 5.11 Emil Jakob Haas Kennkarte.
Source: Central Archive for the Study of the History of the Jews in Germany.

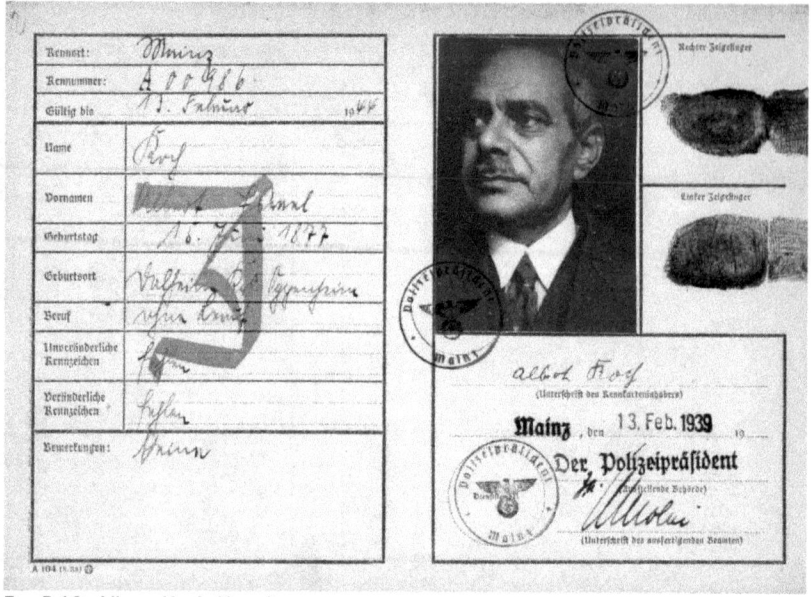

Fig. 5.12 Albert Koch Kennkarte.
Source: Central Archive for the Study of the History of the Jews in Germany.

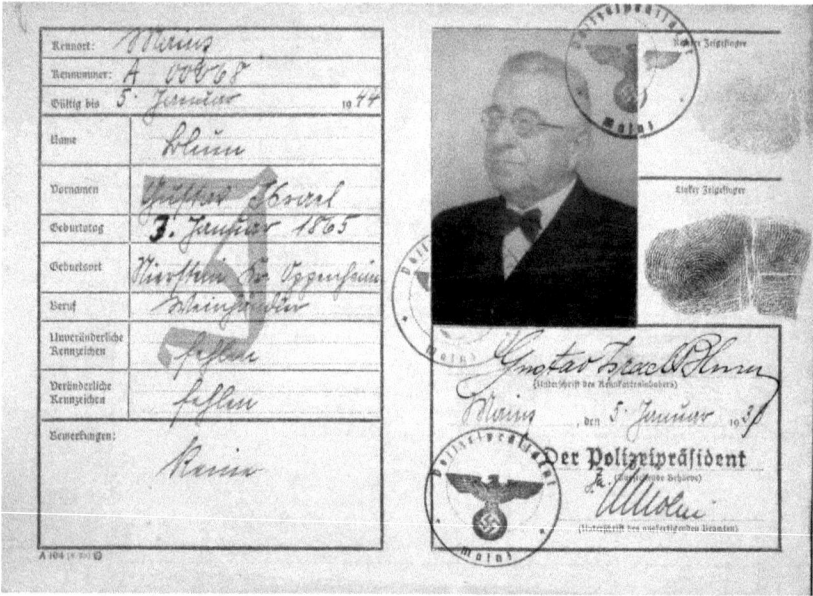

Fig. 5.13 Gustav Blum Kennkarte.
Source: Central Archive for the Study of the History of the Jews in Germany.

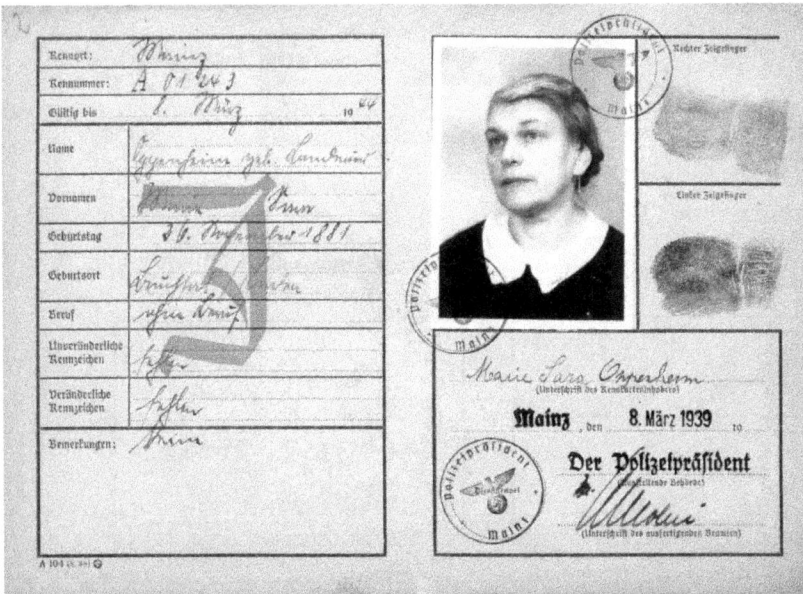

Fig. 5.14 Marie Oppenheim (née Landauer) Kennkarte.
Source: Central Archive for the Study of the History of the Jews in Germany.

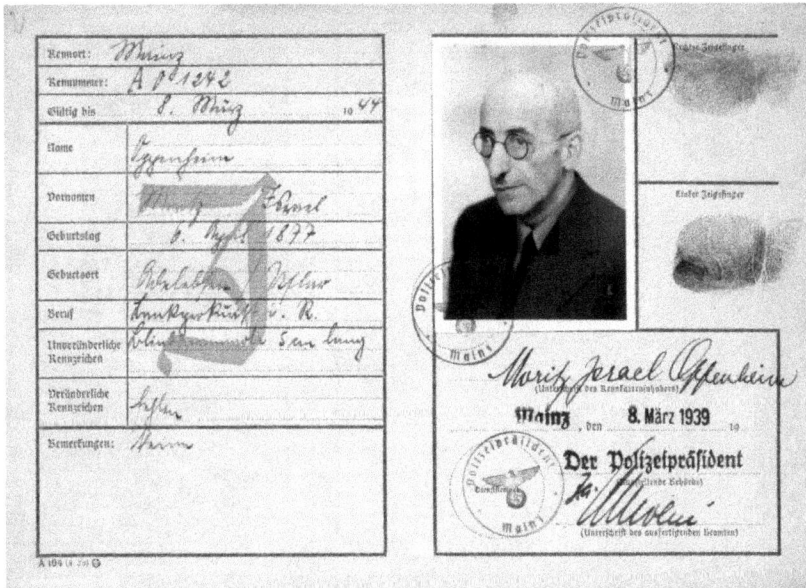

Fig. 5.15 Moritz Oppenheim Kennkarte.
Source: Central Archive for the Study of the History of the Jews in Germany.

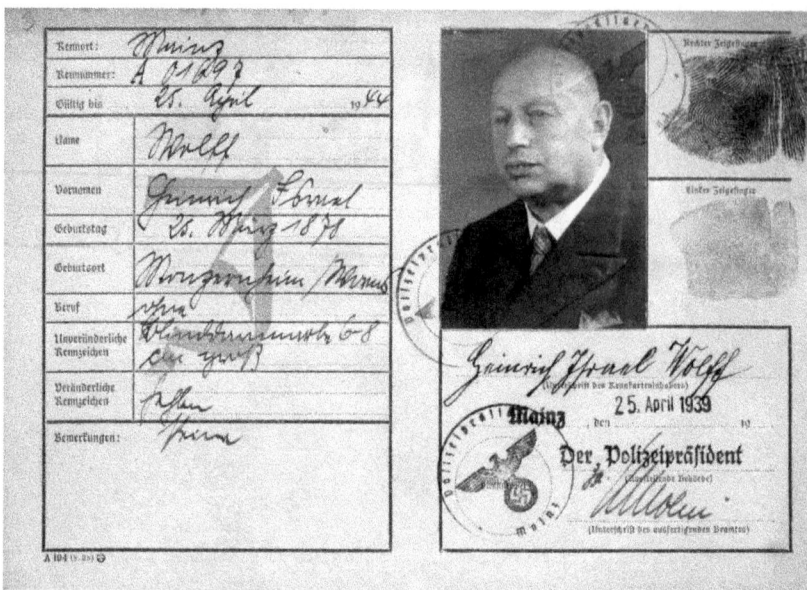

Fig. 5.16 Heinrich Wolff Kennkarte.
Source: Central Archive for the Study of the History of the Jews in Germany.

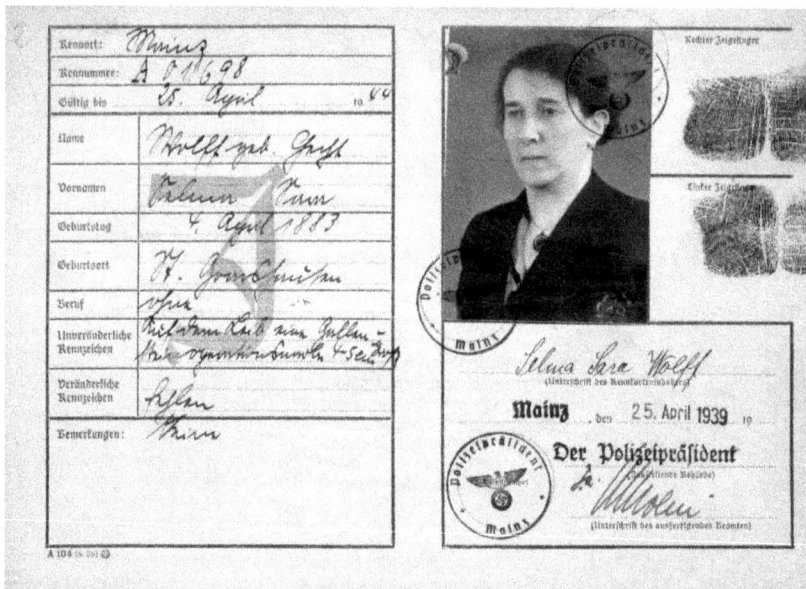

Fig. 5.17 Selma Wolff (née Hecht) Kennkarte.
Source: Central Archive for the Study of the History of the Jews in Germany.

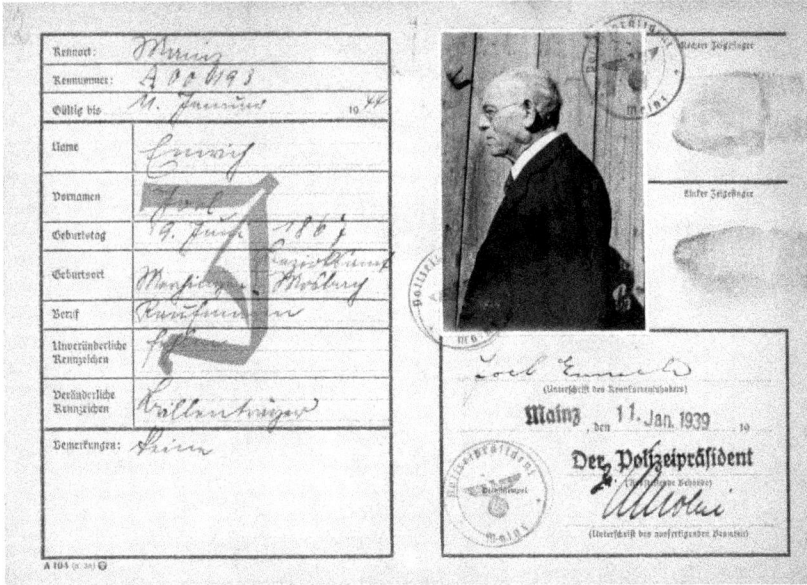

Fig. 5.18 Joel Emrich Kennkarte.
Source: Central Archive for the Study of the History of the Jews in Germany.

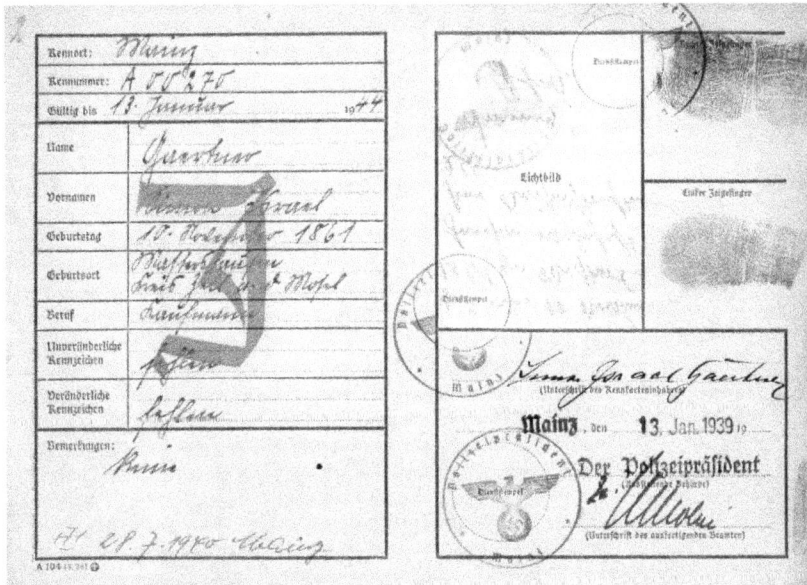

Fig. 5.19 Simon Gaertner Kennkarte.
Source: Central Archive for the Study of the History of the Jews in Germany.

Fig. 5.20 Simon and Juliane Gaertner's Grave,
New Jewish Cemetery Mainz. Source: Michael S.
Phillips Archive.

Fig. 5.21 Stolperstein Outside 24 Kaiserstrasse.
Photo by Nixnubix via Wikipedia.org.

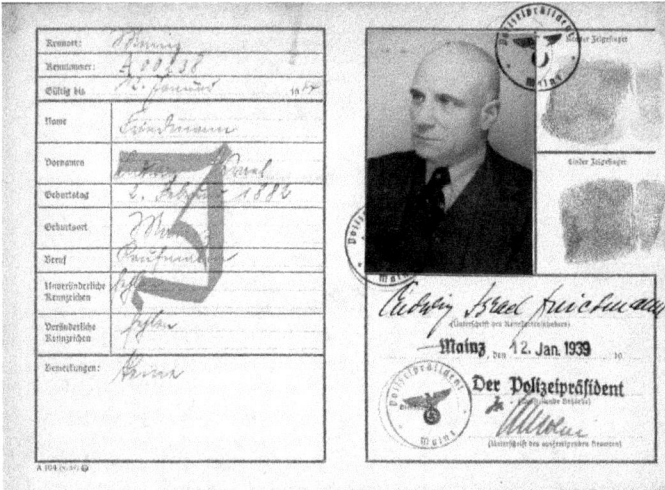

Fig. 5.22 Ludwig Friedman Kennkarte. Source: Central Archive for the Study of the History of the Jews in Germany.

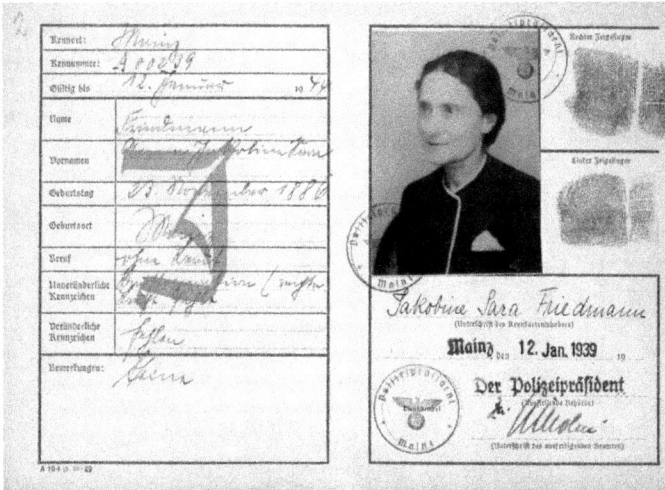

Fig. 5.23 Anna Jakobine Friedmann. Source: Central Archive for the Study of the History of the Jews in Germany.

Fig. 5.24 Albert Fried Kennkarte. Source: Central Archive for the Study of the History of the Jews in Germany.

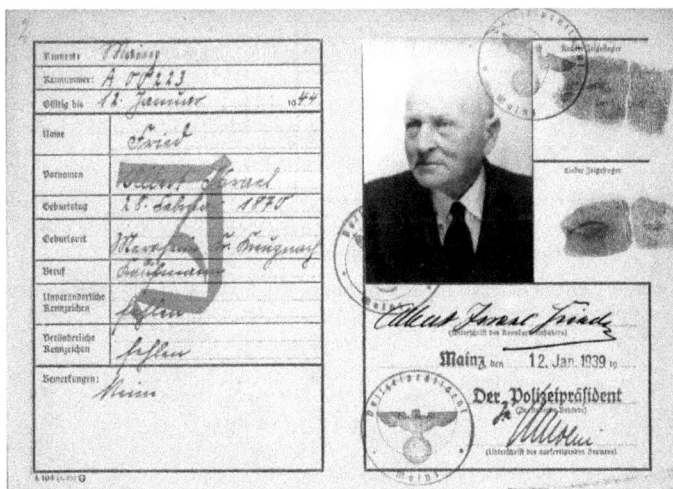

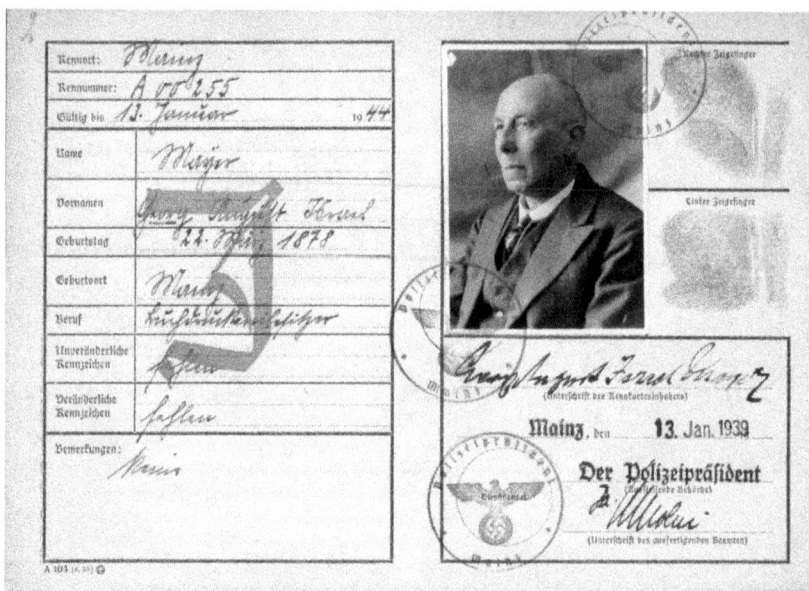

Fig. 5.25 Georg August Mayer Kennkarte.
Source: Central Archive for the Study of the History of the Jews in Germany.

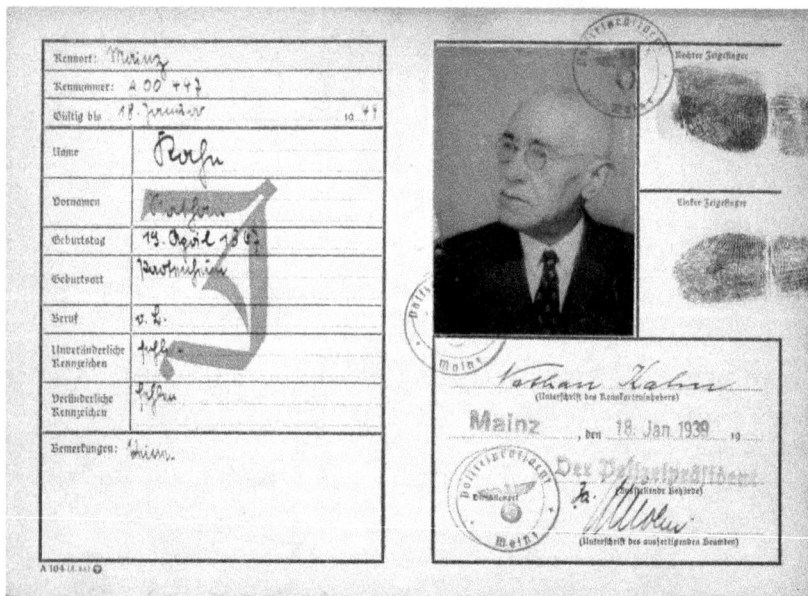

Fig. 5.26 Arthur Nathan Kahn Kennkarte.
Source: Central Archive for the Study of the History of the Jews in Germany.

Fig. 5.27 Ingeborg Henlein Kennkarte.
Source: Central Archive for the Study of the History of the Jews in Germany.

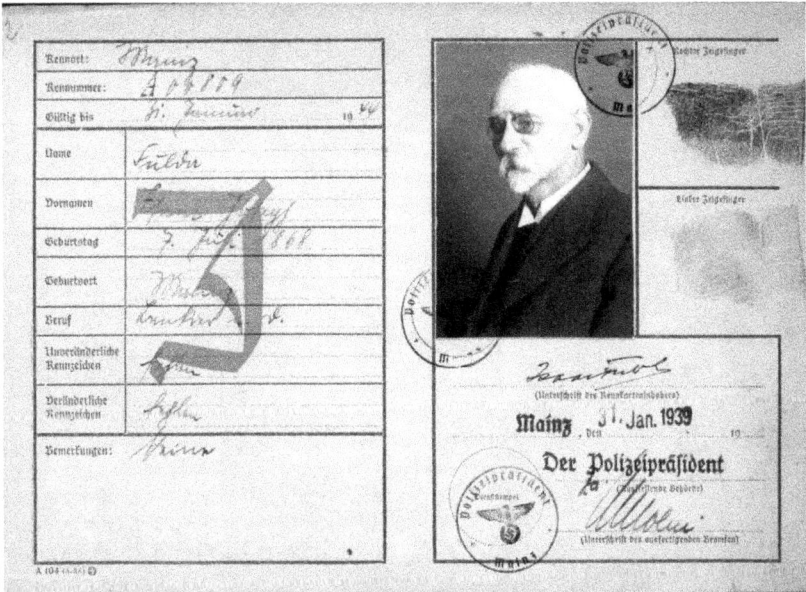

Fig. 5.28 Isaac Joseph Fulda Kennkarte.
Source: Central Archive for the Study of the History of the Jews in Germany.

Fig. 5.29 Fulda Family Stolpersteine, 38 Kaiserstrasse. The stones were laid in a ceremony on 18 February 2014. Photo by Nixnubix via Wikipedia.org.

Fig. 5.30 38 Kaiserstrasse. Source: Michael S. Philips Archive.

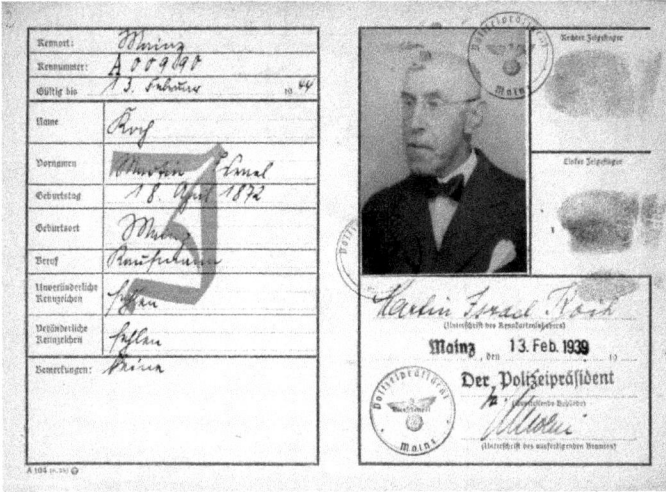

Fig. 5.31 Martin Koch Kennkarte. Source: Central Archive for the Study of the History of the Jews in Germany.

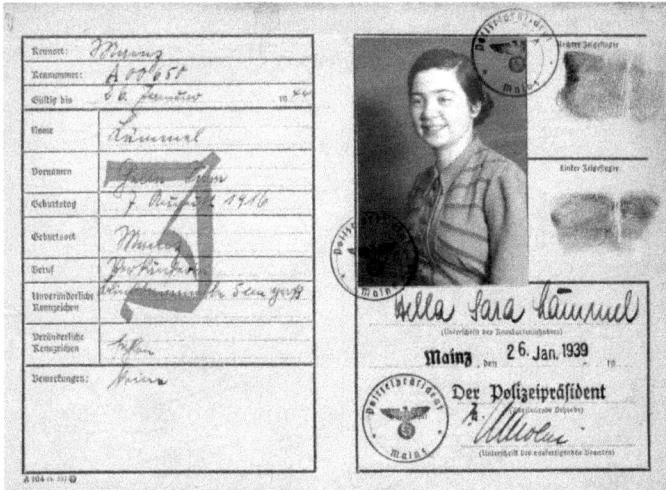

Fig. 5.32 Hella Lämmel Kennkarte. Source: Central Archive for the Study of the History of the Jews in Germany.

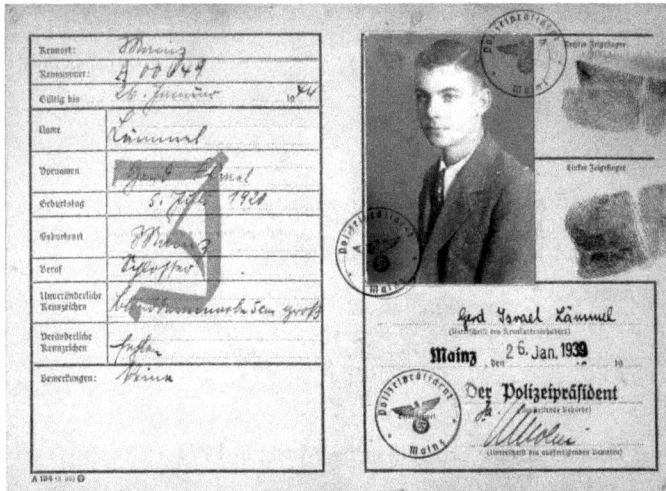

Fig. 5.33 Gerd Lämmel Kennkarte. Source: Central Archive for the Study of the History of the Jews in Germany.

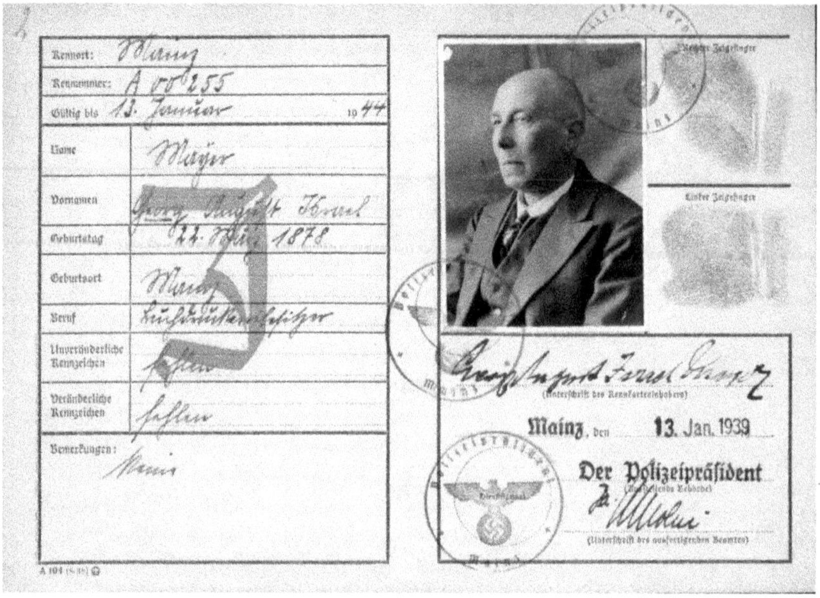

Kennort: Mainz
Kennnummer: A 00255
Gültig bis 13. Januar 1944
Name Mayer
Vornamen
Geburtstag
Geburtsort Mainz
Beruf
Unveränderliche Kennzeichen fehlen
Veränderliche Kennzeichen fehlen
Bemerkungen:

Rechter Zeigefinger
Linker Zeigefinger
(Unterschrift des Kennkarteninhabers)
Mainz, den 13. Jan. 1939
Der Polizeipräsident
(ausfertigende Behörde)
(Unterschrift des ausfertigenden Beamten)

Fig. 5.34 Fritz Siegfried Salomon Kennkarte.
Source: Central Archive for the Study of the History of the Jews in Germany.

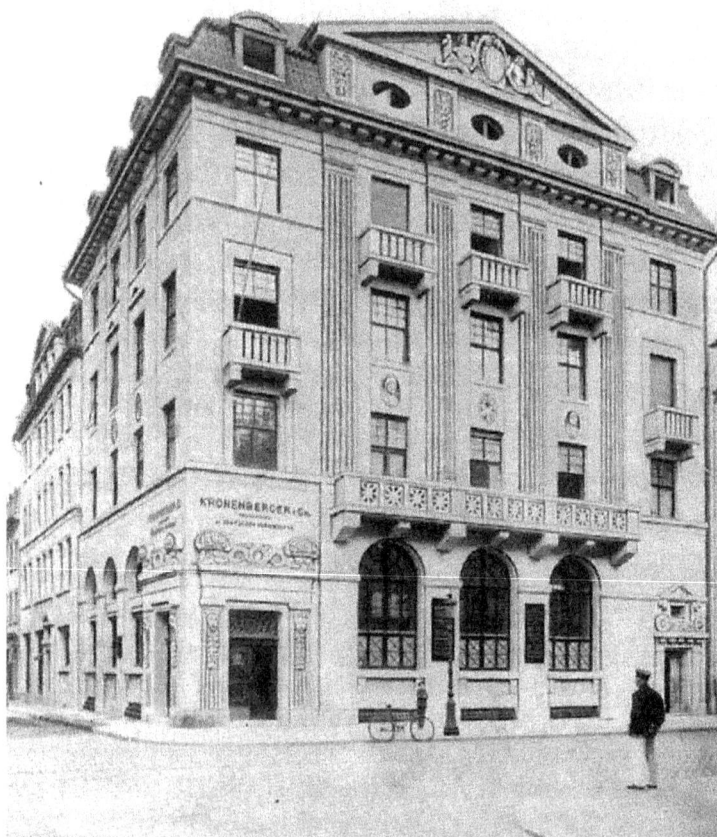

Fig. 5.35 Kronenberger Bank at 35-37 Grosse Bleiche, Mainz in 1911.
Source: unknown, public domain.

Fig. 5.36 Dr. Moritz Karl Goldschmidt Kennkarte.
Source: Central Archive for the Study of the History of the Jews in Germany.

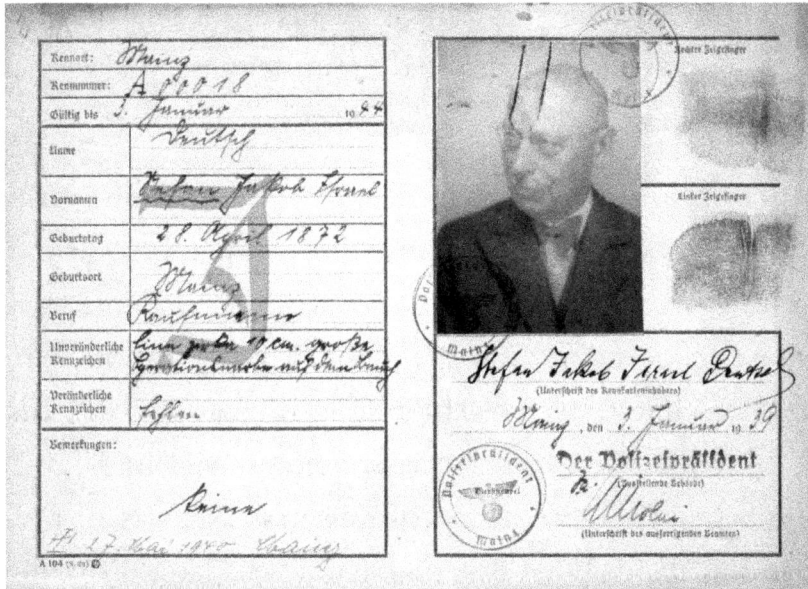

Fig. 5.37 Stefan Jacob Deutsch Kennkarte.
Source: Central Archive for the Study of the History of the Jews in Germany.

Chapter 6. The Survivors

Like many families on Kaiserstrasse, my own was split between those who managed to escape the murderous Nazi regime, like my grandmother Milly, my mother Anneliese and uncle Max Walter, and those that got caught in the Nazi net (even though they may have thought they had found sanctuary)—like Milly's mother Auguste, sister Anny and brother Karl and his wife Sonja and their little boy Joe.

I can imagine planning an escape from Germany—where to go, the route to take, what to take, getting the paperwork needed from a regime that was enthusiastically hostile—was desperately nerve-racking. In the case of my grandmother, she had great friends in England already in the form of sisters Alice Morreau and Berthe Goetz who helped her enormously. Crucially, they provided sponsorship to Milly and her children, as well as emotional and practical support. My grandmother also had the money needed to pay for a German exit visa.

For those who did manage to flee, their destinations varied. My research has largely focused on those that escaped in 1939 and after. By the end of the Second World War, former residents of Kaiserstrasse were scattered around the globe. My grandmother made a home for herself and her two children in England. So did Elisabeth Gabriel (b. 1899) of 84 Kaiserstrasse, who arrived in August 1939. Charlotte Schad (b. 1920), from 29 Kaiserstrasse, was 19 when she arrived in the UK in 1939. She married a year later. Fritz (b. 1860) and Lilly Valfer (b. 1876) and Karola Goldstein (b. 1920)—recorded at the same house, number 29—also arrived in the UK in 1939, as did Gertrude Mayer (b. 1905) of 94 Kaiserstrasse and Bernhard Kahn (b. 1928) and Doris Kahn (b 1924), who were probably siblings and lived at number 96.

For many, the UK was a transit point en route to a destination far from war-torn Europe. Reaching America—which did not enter the War until December 1941—was the objective for most Jews seeking safety, and Kaiserstrasse residents were no exception. However, under the US immigration quota system, by June 1939, the waiting list for Germans seeking to immigrate to the US had reached more than 300,000—more than double the year before. In 1939, the US government issued the entire German quota of just under 30,000 visas.[88]

Those who were successful had been made to jump through bureaucratic hoops to obtain exit and transit permissions, supply identity paperwork, police reports and financial affidavits, and to secure the funds to have a ticket in hand, all at a time of escalating persecution, discrimination and exclusion from public life.[89] They had also to find a US sponsor willing to put up cash, if need be to secure their visa.

The Sichels, my grandmother's neighbours at 26, 28 and 30 Kaiserstrasse, who were also active in the wine trade, all transited through the UK on their way to the US. Eugen (b. 1881) Sichel, his wife Franziska (b. 1938, née Loeb,) and their children Peter (b. 1922) and Ruth (b. 1920) arrived in England in 1938 before travelling—I suspect—by ship to the US. Peter Sichel served as an officer in the US Army and returned to Mainz in 1945 as part of the liberating forces, as detailed in his book.[90] Another Kaiserstrasse resident, Edgar Allmeier (b. 1912) of number 21 also served in the US military and settled in the US after the war. He died in Philadelphia in 1979.

The family of Ernst Mayer (b. 1878), Bernhard Albert Mayer's cousin and colleague at the Martin Mayer jewellery business along with his brother Albert Mayer (b. 1874), lived at number 24 Kaiserstrasse. Ernst also managed the family's brewery, Sonnenbrauerei, before it was 'aryanized' in 1938. Ernst committed suicide in March 1939 and is buried on the New Jewish Cemetery. Records show that his wife Emmy Mayer (b. 1893, née Reitzenstein) arrived in England in 1939. Their daughter Liselotte (b. 1913) also arrived safely in England before travelling on to the US.

Eugene (b. 1876) and Ida Koch (b. 1893) of 38 Kaiserstrasse arrived in the US in May 1939, as did Johanna Mayer (b.1886, née Kapp) of number 55, and Alex Abraham (b. 1891) and Hedwig Abraham (b. 1890, née Mayer) of 56 Kaiserstrasse.

The Blums of 48 Kaiserstrasse, Willy (b. 1886), Camille (b. 1864, née Sichel) and their sons Richard (b. 1889) and Walter (b. 1893), were another wine merchant family. Willy, Camille and Walter arrived in the UK in June 1939, followed by Richard on 29 August 1939. Records show that both Richard and Walter petitioned to become US citizens. Richard's naturalisation application made in Chicago describes him as a wine and liquor salesman with grey hair, blue eyes and a ruddy complexion.

Also in August 1939, Emma Irma Michel (b. 1884, née Altschul) arrived in New York. Emma had been living at 29 Kaiserstrasse, but apparently not with her daughter Erna (b. 1906), who arrived in New York from Hamburg in September 1937, or her divorced husband, Julius Isaak Michel (b. 1877). Julius was deported to Theresienstadt in September 1942 and murdered on 6 May 1944 in Auschwitz. By 1940, Emma and Erna lived together in Chicago, where Emma died in June 1942. Emma's sister Karoline 'Carola' Weis (b. 1879, née Altschul) also lived at 29 Kaiserstrasse for a short period. She was deported from Frankfurt/Main to Sobibor in June 1942.

Selma Löb (b. 1877) of number 82 arrived in the US in November that year. She was followed in February 1940, by Alfred Stern (b. 1895)

and Erna Stern (b. 1901, née Sanders) of 94 Kaiserstrasse. I assume
they were married. Emma Pintus (b. 1871, née Reinach) of 15 Kaiserstrasse arrived in New York on 13 April 1940 on the SS Westerland
from Antwerp. Selma Stern (b. 1893, née Mayer) of 19 Kaiserstrasse
also arrived in April 1940. Max Franz Herz (b. 1902) and Rosemarie
Herz (b. 1915, née Brinitzer) of 35 Kaiserstrasse arrived in England
in August 1939 before travelling on to New York, where they also
arrived in April 1940.

The Gaertners of 94 Kaiserstrasse, Ernst Willy (b. 1891) and Johanna (b. 1896, née Oppenheimer) arrived in August 1940 in Seattle.
Elsbeth Gaertner (1924) had already arrived in the UK in July 1939
before she travelled on to New York in June 1940. Prior to leaving,
Ernst was rescued from Gestapo detention by his elderly mother
Juliane (b. 1859)—who would have been around 80 at the time and
who demanded his release saying she had given two sons to Germany in the First World War and was not prepared to lose another.[91]
Juliane died in Theresienstadt despite her son's efforts, made from
abroad, to save her.[92]

Ludwig Goldschmidt (b. 1882) who owned 31 Kaiserstrasse, the
large property the Gestapo took over as their Mainz HQ, arrived
in New York in late August 1940. Records show his wife Klara Goldschmidt (b. 1890) arrived in the UK in 1939 before travelling on to the
US in August 1940. Their daughter Liselotte Goldschmidt (b. 1919)
arrived in England in 1939, while Heinz Goldschmidt (b. 1925), their
son, arrived in the Netherlands in 1939. Lily Goldschmidt (b. 1902)
of 82 Kaiserstrasse arrived in England in July 1939. She appears to
have lived there for the duration of the war before departing for
New York, where she arrived in May 1946.

Dr Adolf Lekisch (b. 1878) and Nanette Lekisch (b. 1888, née Fulda) of number 29 arrived in the US in January 1941. Auguste Victoria

Marx (b. 1915) of 55 Kaiserstrasse arrived a month later. Albert Mann (b. 1880) and his wife Martha Mann (b. 1891, née Lorch) of 8 Kaiserstrasse arrived in New York the following year. Ludwig (b. 1900) and Ella 'Ellen' Samson (b 1885) arrived in New York in late December 1940. They had lived at 94 Kaiserstrasse.

Some headed first for Sweden, before travelling to the US. Kurt Johann Mayer (b. 1917), Ernst and Emmy Mayer's son, had left Mainz in 1938 headed for Denmark, then Sweden, then the US. Katharina Klara Nathan (b. 1922) of 86 Kaiserstrasse was half Jewish. She headed for Sweden where she gained citizenship before moving to the US in 1962. Her Jewish father Erich Dagobert Nathan (b. 1887) fled to Sweden, where he died in 1944.

And then others, perhaps desperate to leave Germany and unable to wait any longer for their US quota number to come up, were forced to take a more circuitous route to get there. The Scheuer family of 29 Kaiserstrasse—Walter Karl Scheuer (b. 1896), his wife Gertrude Scheuer (b. 1902, née Lebrecht), their daughter Ruth (b. 1930) and son Bernd (b. 1932) had visas for Chile but there was no direct passage after the war had started. Therefore, they travelled first to China on the Trans-Siberian Railway, then through Korea before catching a boat to Japan where, after a short stay, they boarded another boat destined for the US. They were not allowed to disembark at Seattle. And as Chile refused to let Jews go ashore the Scheuer family ended up in Mexico where the parents stayed for the rest of their lives. After the war, their son emigrated to Israel while his sister went to the US. The Heidenheimers of number 82, Albert (b. 1886) and Eva (b. 1893, née Lebrecht) also detoured to Japan before making it to Seattle in July 1940, where they were joined later by their daughter Margret (b. 1925) and their son Willy (b. 1928), who had arrived in England in June 1939 on the kindertransport.

The Rosenthal family at number 27 had planned to leave Germany for years.[93] Salomon 'Sally' Rosenthal (b. 1891) had owned a prosperous butcher's business before the 1933 boycott of Jewish enterprises, after which the family moved from Gross-Gerau to Mainz[94] and he tried to make a living in the wine trade. However, the family's US quota number was high, which meant Sally, his wife Lina Rosenthal (b. 1896, née Seelig) and daughter Renate (b. 1926) had to wait.[95] Their home at number 27 was attacked during Kristallnacht.[96] However, it was the German invasion of Poland that prompted their departure for Bolivia via the Netherlands, where they boarded a ship. They disembarked at Arica in Chile in November 1939 before continuing on to La Paz by train. Once they were settled in Bolivia, the family re-established a butchery business.[97] Renate later moved to New Jersey in the US.[98]

The Rosenthals were far from alone in settling—at least for a while—in South America, although once the war began, immigration regimes there were not much friendlier than the US.[99] Lischen Richart (b. 1971, née Kaufmann) of 84 Kaiserstrasse arrived in Argentina in February 1939. She was followed by Rosel Katzenstein (b. 1878) of number 21, who arrived in March 1941. Rosa Mayer (b. 1876) left 26 Kaiserstrasse and arrived in Argentina in May that year, and Fritz Wolf-Deutsch (b. 1900) of 19 Kaiserstrasse arrived there in December 1939.

Also from number 21, Otto Abraham (b. 1895) and his wife Paula Abraham (b. 1898, née Marx) arrived in the Dominican Republic in August 1939. From number 27, Amalie Frost (b. 1878, née Gutenstein) arrived in Bolivia in February 1940, followed by Sofie Maas (b. 1873) from number 51 in March. Fanny Liebenstein (b. 1886, née Lieber), her nephew Justin Liebenstein (b. 1873) and Amalie Schmelzer (b. 1872, née Lieber) all arrived in Montevideo, Uruguay in April 1941.

Other destinations included neighbouring Switzerland, which perhaps served as a base while refugees made other plans. The lawyer Paul Simon (b. 1884), owner of the house 21 Kaiserstrasse, his (second) wife Sofie Simon (b. 1893, née Frank), and their children Johannes (b. 1925) and Raimund (b. 1929) made it to Switzerland in 1939. In May 1938 Louise Helena Fulda (b. 1865, née Ullmann) of number 29 left for South Africa. According to my research, only two Kaiserstrasse residents headed for Canada: Otto (b. 1885) and Lilly Neumann (b. 1893), who arrived there in 1939.

Privileged Mixed Marriage

A few Kaiserstrasse residents with Jewish heritage met criteria that excluded them from extermination.[100] Although his paternal lineage was Jewish, Karl Joseph Wolf (b. 1880) of 94 Kaiserstrasse survived the war because he was considered Catholic. He died in Mainz in 1962. His Jewish father Lucian Wolf (b. 1844) had converted upon marrying a Catholic woman. As half Jewish, Karl and his brothers Ludwig Joseph (1877-1944) and Bruno (1878-1971) suffered during the Nazi years. They lost their jobs and their dignity, according to Elaine Holden, the wife of a Wolf family member. But, as Holden remarked in an email to me, they did at least keep their lives.

Hedwig Heinrich (b. 1877, née Steinhardt) lived at 25 Kaiserstrasse. According to research conducted by Reinhard Frenzel, Hedwig was born Jewish but was afforded 'privileged mixed marriage' status because she was baptised Catholic and in 1900 married a non-Jew, Friedrich Joseph Heinrich (b. 1865). She was not forced to join the Reich Association for Jews in Germany or wear a yellow star. The couple had three children: Friedrich 'Fritz' Heinrich (1902-1991), Carl-Ernst (1907-2006] and Hanna (1905-1994], according to Fritz's grandson Tim Hall, who told me that his grandparents talked little about the war. For them it was a sad time to be alive. Fritz was forced to work in a labour camp near Lahr in Luxembourg that was liberated by the US Army following the Battle of the Bulge. His wife Hedwig said she survived because American bombing destroyed the train lines. Tim said his mother was nine when the war ended and survived as she was hidden in the countryside.

The Kern family lived at 20 Horst-Wessel-Platz, formerly 20 Kaiserstrasse. This was the same building as the Haas family's, but the direction their lives would take was quite different. Ludwig Kern (b. 1903) was a Protestant, who married Johanna Martha Barbara Jourdan (b. 1898) around 1927, who was half Jewish. Johanna's father Adolf was Jewish by birth, but baptised as a Catholic and her mother Barbara appears to have been Catholic and Johanna was brought up as such. Ludwig, Johanna and their daughter Margot Barbara Johanna Kern (b. 1928) all survived the war under the rules of 'privileged mixed marriage'. Margot was considered a 'quarter-Jew' according to the records of the Frauenlob-Gymnasium, where she enrolled in 1939.

Eleanor Marx (b. 1871, née Levy) who appears on the Oppenheim list of Jews registered at number 27 Kaiserstrasse survived the war with at least one of her daughters Marie Marx (b. 1906) and two sons Walter and Werner. How is unknown to me. Like so much information on individuals who suffered during the Holocaust, exact details are hard to find. Eleanor died in Mönchengladbach in Germany in 1953, confirmed by Marie who died in Laubach in 1992 and the archives at Aachen, the town where Eleanor had married cloth manufacturer Ernst Marx in 1896.

Fig. 6.1 Fig. 6.1 Ludwig and Klara Goldschmidt (back row, fourth and fifth from left) at a family party, c. 1914. Ludwig's cousin, Siegmund Neugarten, is at back left with daughter Trude; his aunt, Lina Goldschmidt, is in the second row, third from left. Klara's parents, the Wertheimers, are at back right. Courtesy of Christopher Burnton.

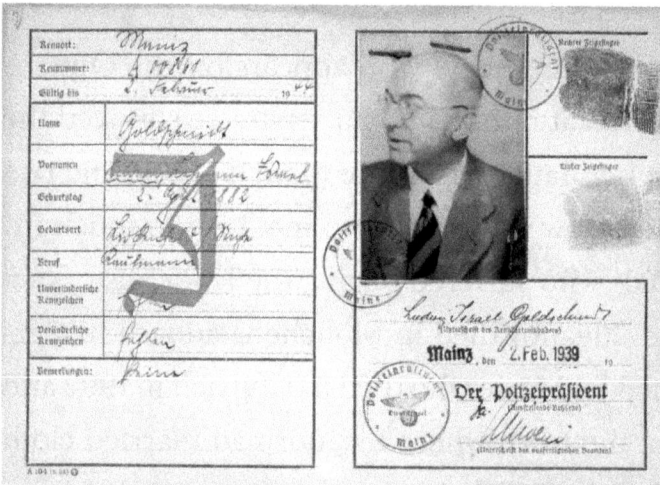

Fig. 6.2 Ludwig Goldschmidt kennkarte. The Goldschmidt family had lived at 31 Kaiserstrasse before they fled Germany and the house became Gestapo headquarters. The notes on the card suggest the original was confiscated at the border. Source: Central Archive for the Study of the History of the Jews in Germany.

Form No. 1   —10

COMMONWEALTH OF PENNSYLVANIA
WORLD WAR II VETERANS' COMPENSATION BUREAU

APPLICATION FOR WORLD WAR II COMPENSATION—TO BE USED BY HONORABLY
DISCHARGED VETERAN OR PERSON STILL IN SERVICE

IMPORTANT—Before Filling Out This Form Study it Carefully.
Read and Follow Instructions—Print Plainly in Ink or Use Typewriter. DO NOT
Use Pencil—All Signatures Must Be in Ink.

Applicant Must Not Write In Space Below

FEB 28 1950

Date Application Was Received

1—Name of Applicant.

ALLMEIER   EDGAR   H.
Last   First   Middle or Initial

Batch Control Number

64533

2—Address to Which CHECK and MAIL is to be Sent.

1136 So. 47th Street   PHILADELPHIA, 43, Phila.   PA.
House No. St. R. D. P. O. Box   City or Town   County   State

Active Domestic Service

Months 10 $ 100
Days $
Amount Due $

3—Date and Place of Birth.

Aug. 28. 1912   MUELHEIM(Moselle)   GERMANY
Month Day Year   City or Town   County   State

4—Name Under Which Applicant Served In World War II.

"SAME NAME"
Last   First   Middle or Initial

Active Foreign Service

Months 0 $
Days $
Amount Due $

5—Date of Beginning and Date of Ending of Each Period of Service Between December 7, 1941 and March 2, 1946 (Both Dates Inclusive) During Which Applicant Was In DOMESTIC SERVICE.

Total Amt. Due $ 100

Domestic Service

Nov. 13. 1942   9-41   Sept. 23. 1943
Date of Beginning   Date of Ending

Audited By
Service Computed By
Amounts Extended by

6—Date of Beginning and Date of Ending of Each Period of Service Between December 7, 1941 and March 2, 1946 (Both Dates Inclusive) During Which Applicant Was In FOREIGN SERVICE.

Date of Beginning   Date of Ending

Approved For Payment
Date SEP 27 1950
For A. G.
For Aud. G.
For S. T.
Application Disapproved
By

7—Date and Place Applicant Entered Active Service.

Dec. 3, 1942   New Cumberland , PA.
Month Day Year   Place

8—Service or Serial Numbers Assigned To Applicant.

Service No's.

Serial No's.   33244936

9—Date and Place Where Applicant Was Separated From Active Service.

Sept. 23. 1943   Camp Maxey, Texas
Month Day Year   Place

10—Is Applicant Now Serving In Armed Forces On Active Duty?   Yes   No   X
If Answer Is YES—Be Sure To Have Certificate Executed And Filed With Application—See Instruction Sheet.

11—Mark "X" Above Name To Indicate Sex And Branch of Service.

X   X
Male   Female   Army   Navy   Marine Corps   Coast Guard   Other—Describe

12—Applicant's Residence At Time of Entry Into Active Service.

23 N. Washington   SHIPPENSBURG, Cumberland   PA.
House No. Street   R. D.   P. O. Box   City or Town   County   State

13—Applicant Was Registered Under Selective Service As Follows.

Local Board No. 3   Harrisburg,   PA.
Draft Board No.   City or Town   County   State

Fig. 6.3 Application for US war service compensation. Edgar Allmeier of 21 Kaiserstrasse joined the US Army in 1942, aged 30. Source: Ancestry.com.

Fig. 6.4 Dr Adolf Lekisch Kennkarte.
Despite strict US visa quotas and numerous bureaucratic hurdles, as well as the
perils of transatlantic travel, Dr Lekisch and his wife Nanette arrived in the US in
early 1941. They had lived at 29 Kaiserstrasse. Source: Central Archive for the Study
of the History of the Jews in Germany.

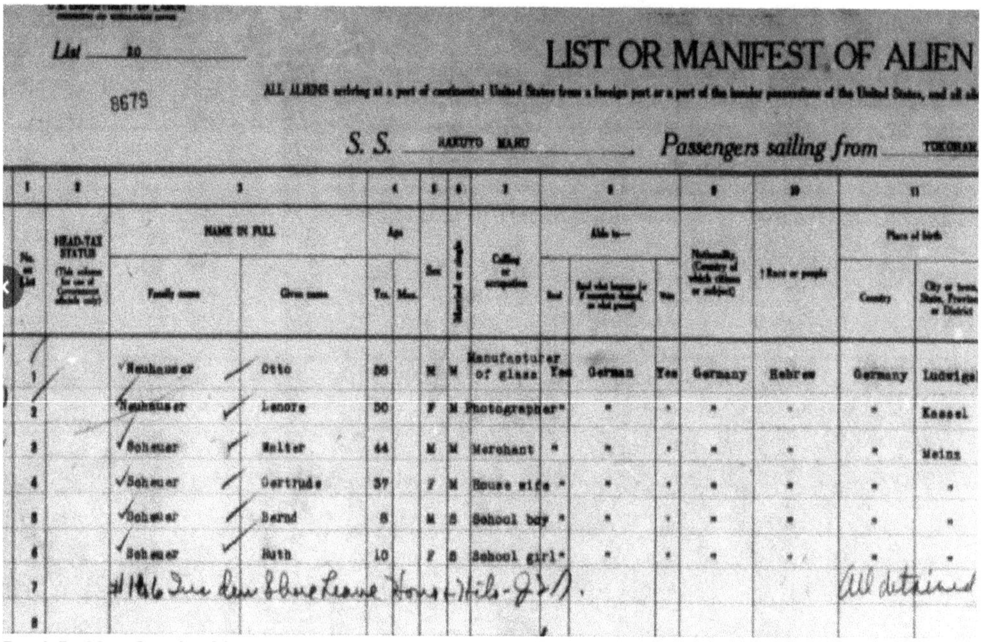

Fig. 6.5 Manifest for SS Rakuyo Maru.
Passengers sailing from Tokyo to Seattle include the Scheuer family of 29 Kaiserstrasse.
Source: Ancestry.com.

-49-

ORIGINAL
(To be retained by
Clerk of Court)

UNITED STATES OF AMERICA

No. 308724

PETITION FOR NATURALIZATION

[Under General Provisions of the Nationality Act of 1940 (Public, No. 853, 76th Cong.)]

To the Honorable the ___DISTRICT___ Court of THE UNITED STATES at ___CHICAGO, ILLINOIS___

This petition for naturalization, hereby made and filed, respectfully shows:

(1) My full, true, and correct name is ___RICHARD BLUM___

(2) My present place of residence is ___Hotel Aragon 5401 Cornell Ave., Chicago, Ill___ (3) My occupation is ___Wine & liquor salesman___

(4) I am ___55___ years old. (5) I was born on ___June 5, 1889___ in ___Mainz, Germany___

(6) My personal description is as follows: Sex ___male___ color ___White___ complexion ___ruddy___ color of eyes ___blue___ color of hair ___grey___ height ___5___ feet ___8___ inches, weight ___158___ pounds, visible distinctive marks ___none___ race ___White___

present nationality ___Germany___ (7) I am ___not___ married; the name of my wife or husband is ___

we were married on ___ at ___

he or she was born at ___ on ___

and entered the United States at ___ on ___ for permanent residence in the United States

and now resides at ___ and was naturalized on ___

at ___ certificate No. ___ or became a citizen by ___

(8) I have ___no___ children; and the name, sex, date and place of birth, and present place of residence of each of said children who is living, are as follows:

(9) My last place of foreign residence was ___Mainz, Germany___ (10) I emigrated to the United States from ___Southampton, England___ (11) My lawful entry for permanent residence in the United States was at ___New York, N.Y___ under the name of ___Richard Blum___

on ___August 29, 1939___ on the ___SS Aquitania___

as shown by the certificate of my arrival attached to this petition.

(12) Since my lawful entry for permanent residence I have ___not___ been absent from the United States, for a period or periods of 6 months or longer, as follows:

DEPARTED FROM THE UNITED STATES			RETURNED TO THE UNITED STATES		
PORT	DATE (Month, day, year)	VESSEL OR OTHER MEANS OF CONVEYANCE	PORT	DATE (Month, day, year)	VESSEL OR OTHER MEANS OF CONVEYANCE

(13) I declared my intention to become a citizen of the United States on ___Dec. 29, 1939___ in the ___U.S. DISTRICT___ Court of ___NORTHERN DIST. OF ILL.___ at ___CHICAGO, ILL.___ (14) It is my intention in good faith to become a citizen of the United States and to renounce absolutely and forever all allegiance and fidelity to any foreign prince, potentate, State, or sovereignty of whom or which at this time I am a subject or citizen, and it is my intention to reside permanently in the United States. (15) I am not, and have not been for the period of at least 10 years immediately preceding the date of this petition, an anarchist; nor a believer in the unlawful damage, injury, or destruction of property, or sabotage; nor a disbeliever in or opposed to organized government; nor a member of or affiliated with any organization or body of persons teaching disbelief in or opposition to organized government. (16) I am able to speak the English language (unless physically unable to do so). (17) I am, and have been during all of the periods required by law, attached to the principles of the Constitution of the United States and well disposed to the good order and happiness of the United States. (18) I have resided continuously in the United States of America for the term of 5 years at least immediately preceding the date of this petition, to wit, since ___Aug. 29, 1939___ and continuously in the State in which this petition is made for the term of 6 months at least immediately preceding the date of this petition, to wit, since ___Sept. 27, 1939___ (19) I have ___not___ heretofore made petition for naturalization: No. ___

on ___ at ___ in the ___

Court, and such petition was dismissed or denied by that Court for the following reasons and causes, to wit: ___ and the cause of such dismissal or denial has since been cured or removed.

(20) Attached hereto and made a part of this, my petition for naturalization, are my declaration of intention to become a citizen of the United States (if such declaration of intention be required by the naturalization law), a certificate of arrival from the Immigration and Naturalization Service of my said lawful entry into the United States for permanent residence (if such certificate of arrival be required by the naturalization law), and the affidavits of at least two verifying witnesses required by law.

(21) Wherefore, I, your petitioner for naturalization, pray that I may be admitted a citizen of the United States of America, and that my name be changed to ___

(22) I, aforesaid petitioner, do swear (affirm) that I know the contents of this petition for naturalization subscribed by me, that the same are true to the best of my own knowledge, except as to matters therein stated to be alleged upon information and belief, and that as to those matters I believe them to be true, and that this petition is signed by me with my full, true name: SO HELP ME GOD.

X ___Richard Blum___

Fig. 6.6 Richard Blum's petition for naturalisation as a US citizen Source: Ancestry.com.

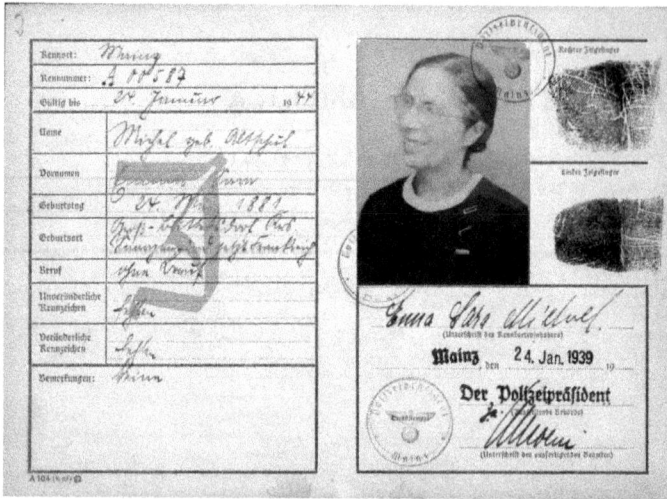

Fig. 6.7 Emma Irma Michel (née Altschul) Kennkarte. Source: Central Archive for the Study of the History of the Jews in Germany.

Fig. 6.8 Julius Isaak Michel Kennkarte. Emma Michel's ex-husband Julius was murdered at Auschwitz. Source: Central Archive for the Study of the History of the Jews in Germany.

Fig. 6.9 Alfred Emil Herz Kennkarte. Source: Central Archive for the Study of the History of the Jews in Germany.

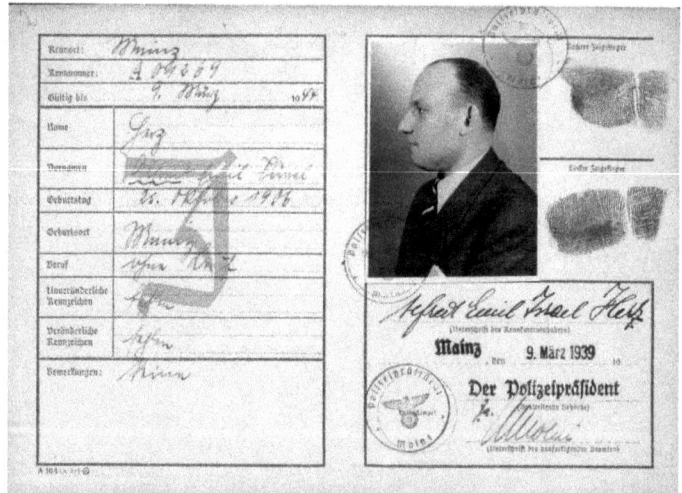

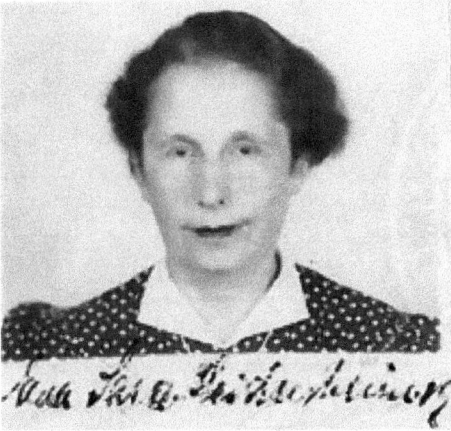

Fig. 6.10 Eva Heidenheimer (née Lebrecht). Eva and her husband Albert arrived in Seattle in 1940 via Japan. Source: US Declaration of Intention; Ancestry.com

Fig. 6.11 Albert Heidenheimer's Declaration of Intention lodged in Los Angeles lists his wife Eva and two children Margret and Willy. Source: Ancestry.com.

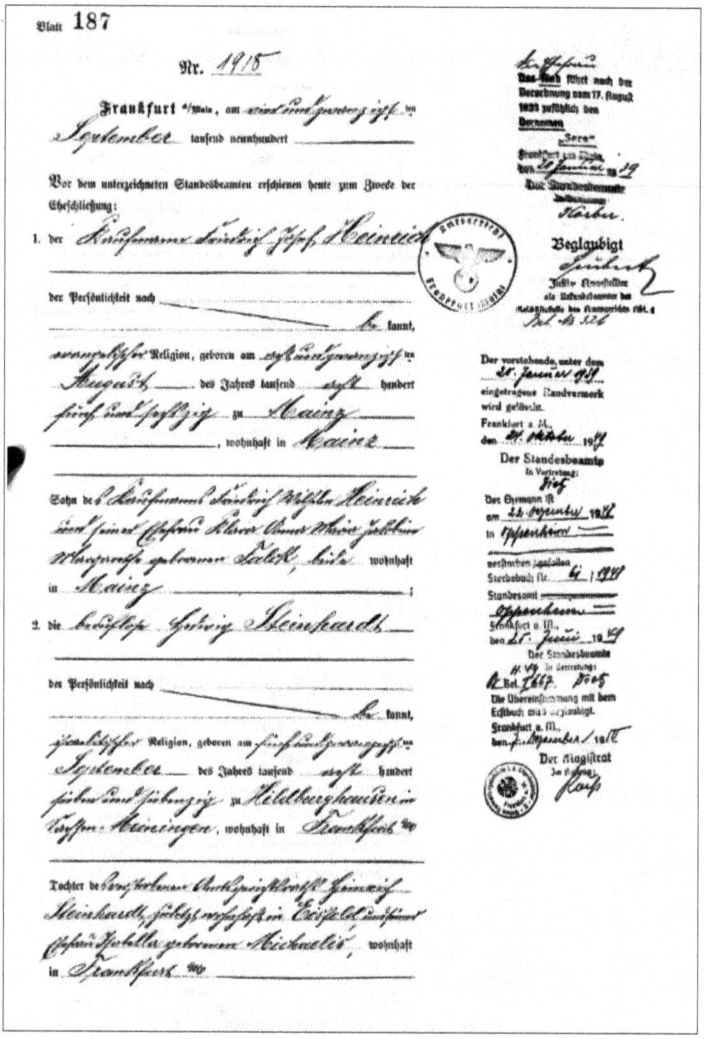

Fig. 6.12 *Privileged Mixed Marriage: Friedrich and Hedwig Heinrich's marriage certificate. The stamps on the marriage certificate show the Nazi authorities examined it to determine whether Hedwig, who was born Jewish, was eligible for privileged mixed marriage status. She survived the war. Although my grandmother was not at all religious, when I was a child she insisted I had been baptised, which I believe was a legacy of that time. Better to be safe than sorry. Source: Ancestry.com.*

Chapter 7. The End

By the end of the Second World War, the Jewish community in Mainz had been destroyed. Its members, Orthodox and Reform, conservative and liberal, segregated and assimilated, had either fled the Nazi regime or been murdered by it. In May 1939, there were only 1,453 members left, most aged 40 or more.[101] By 1948, this already shrunken figure stood at just 80. According to Beate Meyer in her book *A Fatal Balancing Act*, around 3,240 Jews were deported from the Rhine-Hesse region by the Nazis, of which 1,131—more than a third—were from Mainz.[102]

Of those that had made it to safety, I'm not aware of any that returned for good. My grandmother did consider moving back to Germany—after all she had grown up there and lived most of her life in Germany, where she owned property and land and a business—but decided against it. Her family was in England; she had friends and support there in the form of Alice Morreau and Berthe Goetz. Also, life after the war in a defeated Germany was not easy for anyone, and certainly not Jews. Anti-Semitism did not immediately evaporate with the demise of the Nazis.

Today, the Jewish population in Mainz stands at around 1,100, boosted by emigration from the former Soviet Union. A new synagogue and Jewish community centre opened in 2010 on the site of the 1912 Main Synagogue (and its school and museum), which was looted and destroyed on Kristallnacht.[103]

The city remains a focal point of European Jewish history, which dates back to the 10th century. Reflecting its importance, together with the nearby towns of Speyer and Worms, Mainz is part of an application to become a UNESCO World Heritage site.[104] Tourists can pay their respects at the old Judensand graveyard, visit the New

Jewish Cemetery with its Hall of Mourning, be astonished by—at almost 1,000 years old—the oldest datable Jewish gravestone in central Europe which is on display at the Landesmuseum. The museum houses a Judaica collection and a memorial to the Jews deported from Mainz.

A short distance down Mombacher Strasse from the main railway station, just across the road from the Old Jewish Cemetery, sits another important site relevant to the Jews of Mainz. This is the spot where, in 1942 and 1943, hundreds of Jewish people, young and old, waited at the deportation ramp to be taken to their deaths, including residents of Kaiserstrasse. Kaiserstrasse begins a short distance away. Walking down it toward the Rhine you can take in the magnificence of the remaining 19th century mansions while noticing the stolpersteine carefully laid in the pavement to commemorate the Jewish residents who used to live there.

In my research I have documented the fate of around 300 Jews who at one point from 1933-1945 lived on Kaiserstrasse, some because it was their home and others because they were forcibly housed there. I discovered that 118 individuals from this single street were murdered by the Nazi regime. The figure includes those who were deported to transit camps and death centres, as well as those who died in Mainz of starvation, illness or suicide linked to persecution. Seven individuals survived as they fitted the classification of 'non-Jew'. Life would have been a struggle for them too.

Of the murdered, many had been sequestered together in judenhäuser on Kaiserstrasse and around the city and travelled together on the mass deportations to the Piaski ghetto-transit camp in March 1942, and to Theresienstadt and Treblinka at the end of September that year. Others were murdered elsewhere, including Auschwitz,

Belzec, Buchenwald, Majdanek, Plaszow, Sachsenhausen, and Sobibor camps, as well as Krakow and Tarnow.

By my count, 84 Jews left the street from 1933-1939 and 97 managed to leave from 1939 onwards. Most of those headed for the US. Some ended up in unexpected places, such as Shanghai and the Dominican Republic. These were among the few jurisdictions that did not require an entry visa or apply a severely restricted quota regime.

It is striking that these figures relate to just one street in one German city. I put the relatively high number of refugees down to the wealth of the street's pre-war residents that provided them with the means of escape. Jews with more moderate finances living elsewhere in Mainz, Germany or Nazi-occupied Europe would not have been in the same privileged position. My grandmother Milly Schwarz (née Gutmann), mother Anneliese and uncle Max Walter, although displaced and stripped of their assets, possessions and their home and grieving for lost family and friends, were among the lucky ones.[105]

Fig. 7.1   Damage in and around Kaiserstrasse in December 1946. About 80 percent of the buildings in Mainz were destroyed by Allied bombing, shown in medium-dark grey on the map. Source: Mainz City Archives, Reference: BPSP/595 D.

Fig. 7.2 Grosse Bleiche, 1945. The image shows the extent of the damage inflicted on a main street a short distance from Kaiserstrasse. Courtesy of Mainz City Archives.

- Blatt 1 -

Aufstellung der seit 1933 von der Gemeinde Mainz ausgewanderten Juden:

Lfd. No.	Name	geboren am	wo	St.-ang.	letzte Wohng.	ausge-wandert
1.	Abraham, Alex J.	29.10.91	Kl.Winternh.	D.	Kaiserstr.56	Mai 39 USA
2.	Abraham,Hedw.S. geb.Mayer	8.6.90	Oberolm	"	"	" " "
3.	Abraham, Nathan J.	21.3.78	Kriffelbach	"	Große Bl.25	1934 USA
4.	Abraham,Otto J.	12.5.95	Kl.Winternh,	"	Kaiserstr.21	Aug.39 DomR
5.	Abraham, Paula S. geb.Marx	19.5.98	Mehlem	"	"	" " "
6.	Abraham, Philip- pine S.	9.7.58	Obrigheim	"	Stiftswing.12	1938 USA
7.	Adler, Hans Rob.J.	31.10.04	Halle	"	Rheinstr.107	4.9.35 unb.
8.	Adler, Herta S.	2.11.16	Mainz	"	Frauenl.Str.92	Mai 37 USA
9.	Alexander, Leni S. geb.Kronenberger	10.2.99	Mainz	"	Ad.Karr.Str.58	Okt.38 "
10.	Altschul,Berta S. geb.Mann	20.6.82		"	Gr.Bleiche 26	Juli 39 Fr.
11.	Altschul, Camil J.	20.2.78		"	" "	" " "
12.	Baer, Alice S.	23.1.07	Zell	"	Hindenbg.str.38	Dez.39 Holl.
13.	Baer,Bernh.J.	15.7.12	"	"	Sömmering-str.41	Okt.34 Pal
14.	Baer, Bert.J.	18.11.70	Malsch	"	Kaiserstr.82	22.7.36 USA
15.	Baer, Else S. geb.Selig	2.7.85	Hechtsheim	"	"	" " "
16.	Baer. Franz J.	1.12.20	Mainz	"	" 53	12.7.37 "
17.	Baer, Gertr.S.	14.3.11	"	"	" 82	18.10.33 "
18.	Baer. Lina S.	1.6.86	Mergenth.	"	" 53	12.7.37 "
19.	Baer. Max Karl J.	6.8.10	Mainz	"	" "	24.9.33 "
20.	Bamberger, Adelheid Sara	24.2.31	"	"	Neubr.Str.19	1939 Engl.
21.	Bamberger, Benjam.J.	3.6.32	Mainz	"	" "	" "
22.	Bamberger, Julie S.	25.4.11	Ffm.	"	Parkusstr.5	1938 unb.
23.	Bamberger, Moses J.	3.12.02	Kissingen	"	Neubr.Str.19	1939 Engl.
24.	Bamberger, Sal.J.	30.1.37	Mainz	"	" "	" "
25.	Bamberger, Sara	5.8.33	"	"	" "	" "
26.	Bamberger, Seckel J.	11.3.36	Mainz	"	" "	" "

Fig. 7.3 Oppenheim List, page 1.The title of the page is: List of the Jews emigrated since 1933 from the municipality of Mainz. Source: Mainz City Archives, Reference: NL Oppenheim 49,6 Site 141.

Von der Reichsvereinigung der Juden in Deutschland, Abt. "Wanderung, im Jahre 1939 unterstützte Auswanderer, deren letzter inländischer Wohnsitz im Lande Hessen lag."

From the notification of the Jews in Germany: Emigration in the period from 1 January 1938 to 30 September 1940, the last domestic residence in the country was Hessen

L a n d	Jan.	Febr.	März	April	Mai	Juni	Juli	Aug.	Jan.-Aug.	Sept.	Okt.	Nov.	Dez.	Sept.-Dez.	Jan.-Dez.
EUROPA															
Belgien	1	1	-	-	-	-	-	-	1	-	-	-	-	-	1
England	12	11	18	9	9	-	-	1	121	-	-	-	-	-	121
Frankreich	1	1	1	-	1	-	-	-	3	-	-	1	-	-	7
Holland	7	6	6	-	-	-	-	-	25	-	-	-	-	-	25
Italien	-	-	-	-	-	-	-	-	5	-	-	-	17	18	5
Portugal	-	2	-	-	1	5	27	30	3	-	-	-	-	-	3
Schweden	-	1	-	-	1	-	-	5	30	-	-	-	-	-	1
Schweiz	30	-	-	-	-	5	-	1	30	-	-	-	-	-	30
NORDAMERIKA															
U.S.A.	14	3	3	5	3	4	7	11	50	1	12	12	14	39	89
MITTELAMERIKA															
Cuba	-	-	-	-	-	5	1	1	1	-	-	-	-	-	1
Domink.Rep.	-	-	-	-	-	-	-	-	-	-	-	-	-	-	-
SUEDAMERIKA															
Argentinien	4	1	2	-	2	1	9	2	19	-	-	-	-	-	37
Brasilien	-	1	3	-	4	-	2	-	7	-	-	1	-	-	7
Paraguay	-	-	2	-	2	2	1	-	1	-	-	-	-	-	1
AFRIKA															
Rhodesien	-	-	-	-	-	-	-	6	8	-	-	-	-	-	8
Südafrika	-	1	-	8	-	-	-	3	8	-	-	-	-	-	39
ASIEN															
Shanghai	-	-	11	-	13	-	2	-	39	-	-	-	-	-	39
Philippinen	-	1	-	-	1	-	-	-	4	-	-	-	-	-	4
AUSTRALIEN															
Australien	-	-	1	-	1	-	2	-	8	8	-	-	-	-	8
	70	25	47	22	36	21	48	59	328	271	728	800	1591	3390	385
Unterstützte Ausw.insges.	1943	1878	3477	2531	2504	2626	2805	2800	20564	271	728	800	1591	3390	23954
Anteil von Hessen in %:	70	25	47	22	36	21	48	59	328	1	12	13	31	57	385
									1,6%					1,7%	1,6%

Supported emigration in total.

Fig. 7.4 Jewish Emigration from the Hesse Region from January 1938–30 September 1940 by Month. Source: Mainz City Archives, Reference: NL Oppenheim 49,6 Site 197.

Von der Reichsvereinigung der Juden in Deutschland Abt. Wanderung
in der Zeit vom 1.1.1938 – 3o.9.194o unterstützte Auswanderer,
deren letzter inländischer Wohnsitz im Lande Hessen lag.

L a n d	1938	1939	1.1.–3o.9.4o	1.1.38–3o.9.4o
EUROPA				
Belgien	4	1	–	5
England	5	121	–	126
Frankreich	5	3	–	8
Holland	14	25	–	39
Italien	–	5	–	5
Portugal	–	1	–	1
Schweden	–	3	–	3
Schweiz	–	3o	–	3o
NORDAMERIKA				
U.S.A.	211	89	1o9	4o9
" (über Japan)	–	–	22	22
" (über Portugal)	–	–	3	3
MITTELAMERIKA				
Cuba	1	1	–	2
Dominik. Republik	–	1	4	5
Mexiko	2	–	–	2
SUEDAMERIKA				
Argentinien	4o	37	6	83
" (über Japan)	–	–	2	2
Bolivien	–	–	14	14
Brasilien	–	1	3	4
Chile	–	–	1	1
" (über Japan)	–	–	4	4
Columbien	8	–	–	8
Ecuador	3	–	–	3
Paraguay	–	7	–	7
Uruguay	2	–	–	2
AFRIKA				
Rhodesien	–	1	–	1
Südafrika	3	8	6	17
ASIEN				
China (Shanghai)	1	39	1	41
Philippinen	–	4	–	4
AUSTRALIEN				
Australien	1	8	–	9
	3oo	385	175	86o
Unterstützte Auswanderung insges.:	8647	23954	7o62	39663
Anteil von Hessen in %	3,5 %	1,6 %	2,5 %	2,2 %

Fig. 7.5 *Jewish Emigration from the Hesse Region from January 1938–30 September 1940 by Year.*
Source: *Mainz City Archives, Reference: NL Oppenheim 49,6 Site 194.*

Footnotes

Chapter 1. Escape

1 In 1938 $1 = RM 2.49; £1 = RM 12.4 http://www.history.ucsb.edu/faculty/marcuse/projects/currency.htm

2 Peter M F Sichel, The Secrets of My Life: Vintner, Prisoner, Soldier, Spy (Archway Publishing, 2016)

3 Reinhard Frenzel, "Familien Max & Ferdinand Gutmann", Renate Knigge-Tesche and Hedwig Brüchert eds, Der Neue Jüdische Friedhof in Mainz: Biographische Skizzen zu Familien und Personen, die hier ihre Ruhestätte haben, (Verein für Sozialgeschichte Mainz, 2013) p. 118

4 Ibid.

5 Ibid.

6 "Antisemitic Legislation 1933-1939". Holocaust Encyclopaedia, United States Holocaust Memorial Museum (USHMM), https://encyclopedia.ushmm.org/content/en/article/antisemitic-legislation-1933-1939

7 "Riga", Holocaust Encyclopaedia, https://encyclopedia.ushmm.org/content/en/article/riga

8 "Elsbeth Juda: Grit and Glamour", The Jewish Chronicle, 7 March 1918, https://www.thejc.com/culture/culture-diary/elsbeth-juda-grit-and-glamour-at-the-jewish-museum-london-1.460142

9 National Portrait Gallery, London. https://www.npg.org.uk/collections/search/portrait/mw149422/Winston-Churchill?LinkID=mp61695&role=art&rNo=7

Chapter 2. The Jews of Mainz

10 "The Bombing of Mainz in World War II," Wikipedia https://en.wikipedia.org/wiki/Bombing_of_Mainz_in_World_War_II

11 "Jewish Mainz", Tourismus Mainz, https://www.mainz-tourismus.com/en/explore-enjoy/exploring-the-history-of-mainz/jewish-mainz/

12 "ShUM Cities of Speyer, Worms and Mainz", World Heritage Convention, UNESCO, https://whc.unesco.org/en/tentativelists/5975/

13 Ibid.

14 Ibid.

15 Ibid.

16 "Rashi: Rabbi Schlomo Yitzchaki", Nissan Mendel, Chabad, https://www.chabad.org/library/article_cdo/aid/111831/jewish/Rashi-Rabbi-Shlomo-Yitzchaki.htm

17 Beate Meyer, "A Fatal Balancing Act: the Dilemma of the Reich Association of Jews", (Berghahn Books, 2016) pp275-279

18 "Michel Oppenheim", Wikipedia, https://de.wikipedia.org/wiki/Michel_Oppenheim

19 Gudrun Maierhof, "Central Organisations of Jews in Germany 1933-1943", Jewish Women's Archive https://jwa.org/encyclopedia/article/central-organizations-of-jews-in-germany-1933-1943

20 http://www.stolpersteine.eu/en/home/

Chapter 3. Persecution

21 "Mainz." Encyclopaedia Judaica, Encyclopedia.com. (March 17, 2019), https://www.encyclopedia.com/places/germany-scandi-navia-and-central-europe/german-political-geography/mainz

22 "Magenza—the history of Jewish Mainz", Mainz in Rhein-hessen, regionalgeschichte.net, (January 2020) https://www.regionalgeschichte.net/rheinhessen/mainz/einzelaspekte/ma-genza-die-geschichte-des-juedischen-mainz.html

23 Ibid.

24 "Boycott of Jewish Businesses", Holocaust Encyclopedia, https://encyclopedia.ushmm.org/content/en/article/boycott-of-jew-ish-businesses

25 "Nuremberg Race Laws", Holocaust Encyclopedia, https://encyclopedia.ushmm.org/content/en/article/the-nuremberg-race-laws

26 Kristallnacht", Holocaust Encyclopedia, https://encyclopedia.ushmm.org/content/en/article/kristallnacht

27 "Mainz", Encyclopedia Judaica, https://www.encyclopedia.com/places/germany-scandinavia-and-central-europe/german-po-litical-geography/mainz

28 Wannsee Conference", Wikipedia, https://en.wikipedia.org/wiki/Wannsee_Conference

29 "Wannsee Conference and the 'Final Solution'", Holocaust Ency-clopedia, https://encyclopedia.ushmm.org/content/en/article/wannsee-conference-and-the-final-solution

30 "Carl T. Frank: Betrayed by Your Own Tenant", SWR2, https://www.swr.de/swr2/stolpersteine/menschen/frank-carl-theo-

dor/-/id=12117596/did=14186194/nid=12117596/1yvaojo/index.
html

31 Ibid.

32 "Theresienstadt", Holocaust Encyclopedia, https://encyclopedia.
ushmm.org/content/en/article/theresienstadt

33 Ibid.

34 "Carl T. Frank".

35 Renate Knigge-Tesche, "Familie Ladenburg", Der Neue Jüdische
Friedhof, p. 160

36 Ibid., p. 162

37 Ibid.

38 Ibid., p. 163

39 Ibid.

40 Ibid., p. 164

41 Ibid.

42 Ibid.

43 Ibid., p. 165

44 "Antisemitic Legislation", Holocaust Encylopedia, https://
encyclopedia.ushmm.org/content/en/article/antisemitic-legis-
lation-1933-1939

45 Ibid.

46 "Nazi Transit Camps: Malines/Mechelen", Jewish Virtual Library,
https://www.jewishvirtuallibrary.org/malines-mechelen-tran-
sit-camp

47 "Transport, Train Da 14 from Darmstadt, Darmstadt (Darmstadt), Hesse, Germany to Piaski Luterskie, Ghetto, Poland on 21/03/1942", The International Institute for Holocaust Research, Yad Vashem Database, http://db.yadvashem.org/deportation/transportDetails.html?language=en&itemId=5604917

48 Ibid.

49 Ibid.

50 "Law for the Protection of German Blood and German Honor", Holocaust Education & Archive Research Team, http://www.holocaustresearchproject.org/holoprelude/pbgh.html

51 "Victims of the Nazi Era: Nazi Racial Ideology", Holocaust Museum, https://encyclopedia.ushmm.org/content/en/article/victims-of-the-nazi-era-nazi-racial-ideology; "Chart Illustrating the Nuremburg Laws", Holocaust Museum, https://encyclopedia.ushmm.org/content/en/photo/chart-illustrating-the-nuremberg-laws

52 Hedwig Brüchert, "Familien Martin Mayer & Bernhard Albert Mayer", in: Der Neue Jüdische Friedhof, p. 206.

53 Ibid., p. 208

54 Ibid., p. 209

55 Ibid., p. 210

56 Ibid.

57 Ibid.

58 Ibid.

59 Ibid., p. 211

60 Ibid., p. 212

61 Ibid., p. 210

62 "Kindertransport", World Jewish Relief, https://www.
worldjewishrelief.org/about-us/kindertransport?gclid=EAIaI-
QobChMIubqqveeV4QIV5b3tCh2Yng3oEAAYASAAEgKr4vD_
BwE

63 Brüchert, "Familie Martin Mayer", p. 214

Chapter 4. Judenhäuser

64 "Law on Alteration of Family and Personal Names", Holocaust Encyclopaedia, https://www.ushmm.org/learn/
timeline-of-events/1933-1938/law-on-alteration-of-family-
and-personal-names

65 Mainz: A 1000 Years of Jewish History Along the Rhine
(Landesmuseum pamphlet), p. 16

66 "Antisemitic Legislation", Holocaust Encyclopedia,
https://encyclopedia.ushmm.org/content/en/article/
antisemitic-legislation–1933-1939

67 Ibid.

68 Alfred Gottwald & Diana Schulle, Die "Judendeportationen aus
dem Deutschen Reich 1941-1945", (Marix, Wiesbaden 2005)

69 Ibid.

70 Ibid.

71 Ibid.

72 "Mainz: 1000 Years", p. 15

73 Christiane Zehl Romero, "Anna Seghers 1900-1983", Jewish
Women's Archive Encyclopaedia, https://jwa.org/encyclopedia/
article/seghers-anna

74 Ibid.

75 Ibid.

76 Ibid.

77 Ibid.

Chapter 5. The Murdered

78 "Transport, Train Da 14", Yad Vashem Database, http://db.yadvashem.org/deportation/transportDetails.html?language=en&itemId=5604917

79 "Tarnow Ghetto", Holocaust Education, http://www.holocaustresearchproject.org/ghettos/tarnow.html

80 Ibid.

81 "The Nuremberg Laws: Background & Overview", Jewish Virtual Library, https://www.jewishvirtuallibrary.org/background-and-overview-of-the-nuremberg-laws

82 "In Spite of All This: A Portrait of Resistance in the Rhine-Main Area—Gertrude Meyer-Jorgensen", Widerstand, (Widerstand pamphlet, 2008), http://www.widerstand-portrait.de/portraits/gertrude-meyer-jorgensen.html

83 Simone Wagner, "Emigration in the Nazi Era: Gerti Meyer-Jorgensen: A Jewess Returns", Institute for Historical Geography at the University of Mainz e.V. 2001-2019, https://www.auswanderung-rlp.de/emigration-in-der-ns-zeit/gerti-meyer-jorgensen.html

84 Tillmann Krach, "Dr. Karl Goldschmidt", in Der Neue Jüdische Friedhof, p. 111

85 Ibid.

86 Ibid.

87 Ibid.

Chapter 6. The Survivors

88 "Immigration to the United States 1933-41", Holocaust Ency-
    clopedia, https://encyclopedia.ushmm.org/content/en/article/
    immigration-to-the-united-states-1933-41

89 Ibid.

90 Sichel, "The Secrets of My Life: Vintner, Prisoner, Soldier, Spy,"
    p. 6.

91 David Leveille, "Remembering an 80-year old Jewish wom-
    an who marched into the Gestapo to demand the release of
    her son", Public Radio International, https://www.pri.org/
    stories/2015-10-15/remembering-80-year-old-jewish-woman-
    who-marched-gestapo-demand-release-her-son

92 Ibid.

93 Simone Wagner, "Renata Rosenthal—Like a tree without
    roots in a foreign country?", (Institute of History, University
    of Mainz); Renata Schwarz, Von Mainz nach La Paz. Kindheit
    eines jüdischen Mädchens in Deutschland und Flucht nach Bo-
    livien, ed. and translated by Hedwig Brüchert (Sonderheft der
    Mainzer Geschichtsblätter, Verein für Sozialgeschichte Mainz
    e.V.), Mainz 2007

94 "Darmstädter Strasse 43", Stumbling Blocks Guide, https://
    stolpersteine-guide.de/biografie/1155/familie-rosenthal

95 Darmstädter Strasse 43, http://www.erinnerung.org/gg/haeuser/
    da43.html; Renata Schwarz, Von Mainz nach La Paz

96 Ibid.

97 Ibid.

98 Ibid.

99 Refuge in Latin America, Holocaust Encyclopedia, https:// encyclopedia.ushmm.org/content/en/article/refuge-in-lat- in-america

100 Beate Meyer, "The Mixed Marriage: A Guarantee of Survival or a Reflection of German Society during the Nazi Regime?" in Probing the depths of German Antisemitism: German society and the persecution of the Jews, 1933-1941, ed. David Bankier (Berghahn, 2000), p. 60.

Chapter 7. The End

101 "Mainz." The Columbia Encyclopaedia, 6th ed. https://www. encyclopedia.com/places/germany-scandinavia-and-cen- tral-europe/german-political-geography/mainz

102 Meyer, "A Fatal Balance", p. 277

103 Peter Wortsman, "Tracing Jewish History Along the Rhine," The New York Times, 4 September 2014, https://www.nytimes. com/2014/09/07/travel/tracing-jewish-history-along-the- rhine.html

104 https://whc.unesco.org/en/tentativelists/5975/

105 My research has been painstaking and I discovered that in many cases contradictory records exist. If I have inadvertently missed someone who should be included in this book, I apologise to them and their families.

Resources

A *Fatal Balancing Act: the Dilemma of the Reich Association of Jews* by Beate Meyer, (Berghahn Books, 2016)

Ancestry.com

American Joint Distribution Committee Archives

Frauenleben in Magenza, 2015

Central Archive for the Study of the History of the Jews in Germany

City Archives: Aachen, Alzey, Berlin, Köln and Mainz

Der Neue Jüdische Friedhof in Mainz: Biographische Skizzen zu Familien und Personen, die hier ihre Ruhestätte haben, by Renate Knigge-Tesche and Hedwig Brüchert eds (Verein für Sozialgeschichte Mainz, 2013) [Trans: The New Jewish Cemetery in Mainz: biographical sketches of families and people whose resting place is here.]

Die "Judendeportationen" aus dem Deutschen Reich 1941-1945 by Alfred Gottwald & Diana Schulle, (Marix, Wiesbaden 2005)

Encyclopaedia Judaica

Geni.com

Holocaust Encyclopaedia, United States Holocaust Memorial Museum

Holocaust Education & Archive Research Team

Jewish Encyclopaedia

Institute for Historical Geography, University of Mainz

Institute of History, University of Mainz

JewishGen.org

Jewish Women's Archive

Jewish Virtual Library

Mainz Landesmuseum

Michael S. Phillips Archive

Oppenheim Lists, Mainz City Archives

Probing the depths of German Antisemitism: German society and the persecution of the Jews, 1933-1941, ed. David Bankier (Berghahn, 2000)

Public Radio International

regionalgeschichte.net

Stolpersteine Committee of Mainz

State Archives of Latvia

The Jewish Chronicle

The Melbourne Argus

The Memorial Book of the Federal Archives for the Victims of the Persecution of the Jews in Germany (1933-1945)

The National Portrait Gallery

The Secrets of My Life: Vintner, Prisoner, Soldier, Spy by Peter M F Sichel, (Archway Publishing, 2016)

Tourists Centre Mainz

UNESCO

University of California, Santa Barbara, History Department

Wikipedia

Wikimedia Commons

Widerstand

World Jewish Relief

Yad Vashem: Hall of Names; The International Institute for Holocaust Research

Family of Carl Frank, Mainz, c. 1896. Carl and his wife Mathilde are standing back right. Their son Rudolf (sailor suit) is in the second row, second from left. To his right are Carl's parents, Franziska and Nathan. The little girl at front left is Carl's niece Sofie. Courtesy of Roy Jacobson.

Acknowledgements

First and foremost is my most grateful thanks to Reinhard Frenzel, for his friendship and for making this book at all possible. His dedication to detail and dogged research on the Jewish pupils from the Höhere Mädchenschule, now the Frauenlob-Gymnasium, where he had once been a teacher of English, was invaluable. Very little background on anything pre-dating my mother would have been forthcoming without Reinhard's involvement.

I would also like to thank a second Mainz-based historian, Dr Hedwig Brüchert, for her assistance, input and close eye for detail. Background on Auguste Gutmann, née Mayer, was provided by another dedicated researcher—Renate Rosenau from Alzey. Again, thank you.

My gratitude also extends to the Mainz City Archives that provided considerable information on each of the Kaiserstrasse houses and the events affecting all the Jewish inhabitants, and also to various members of the Mainz Stolpersteine committee.

I would also like to thank the numerous individuals worldwide who contributed historical context and confirmation of the Jewish inhabitants of Kaiserstrasse. For many years Laurence Asslinger and I worked together on the Gutmann and Hochschild links that connect both of us. My many thanks for both his friendship and help.

For encouragement and assistance from Christine Thorsrud in Alaska, a descendant of Max Gutmann, I am deeply grateful.

And also for the encouragement and assistance I received from Walter Goetz (pre 1995), who provided much background on his mother and aunt, my grandmother's great friends, Berthe Goetz and Alice Morreau, and from friends Francis, Jane, Randolph and Richard.

My thanks must also include retired architect and current president of the Greenwich Society (London) Ursula Bowyer, who is the daughter of my grandmother's lifelong friend from Mainz, Lily Meyer, née Marx. Ursula introduced me to Sarah Winterbottom and through Sarah, Victoria Robson. Together they have brought this book to life with their journalistic and editing skills.

About the Author

Michael Stowell Phillips was born 16 May 1944 in Mansfield, Nottinghamshire, to Dr Ronald Hugh Stowell Phillips, who was born in Tamil Nadu, India, and Anneliese Schwarz from Greiz, Germany. Following his parents' divorce a year later, Michael was brought up in Guildford, Surrey, by his maternal grandmother, Amalie (Milly) Schwarz (née Gutmann), who had fled Nazi Germany with her children Anneliese and Max Walter Schwarz in 1939.

After obtaining a degree in Special Physics in 1970 from Regent Street Polytechnic, Michael embarked on a career in management. His interest in his family's history was ignited in 1990 when he made his first visit to Greiz, following the fall of the Berlin Wall. Since then, until his death in June 2020, he devoted his time to researching his Jewish roots. Michael leaves behind his wife Elizabeth, two children, and four grandchildren.

Index